222.76

CH   UNDARY

      MW01041260 ...UUL LIBRARY

CHATELECH SECONDARY SCHOOL LIBRARY

012606

DISCARDED

WILDERNESS
PRESERVATION

EARTH • AT • RISK

WILDERNESS PRESERVATION

by Richard Amdur

Introduction by
Russell E. Train

Chairman of
the Board of Directors,
World Wildlife Fund and
the Conservation Foundation

CHELSEA HOUSE PUBLISHERS

new york   philadelphia

CHELSEA HOUSE PUBLISHERS
EDITOR-IN-CHIEF: Richard S. Papale
MANAGING EDITOR: Karyn Gullen Browne
COPY CHIEF: Philip Koslow
PICTURE EDITOR: Adrian G. Allen
ASSISTANT ART DIRECTOR: Howard Brotman
MANUFACTURING DIRECTOR: Gerald Levine
SYSTEMS MANAGER: Lindsey Ottman
PRODUCTION COORDINATOR: Marie Claire Cebrián-Ume

EARTH AT RISK
SENIOR EDITOR: Jake Goldberg

Staff for *Wilderness Preservation*
ASSOCIATE EDITOR: Karen Hammonds
COPY EDITOR: David Carter
EDITORIAL ASSISTANT: Robert Kimball Green
PICTURE RESEARCHER: Villette Harris
SENIOR DESIGNER: Marjorie Zaum
COVER ILLUSTRATION: Vilma Ortiz

Copyright © 1993 by Chelsea House Publishers, a division of
Main Line Book Co. All rights reserved. Printed and bound in
the United States of America.

 This book is printed on recycled paper.

First printing

1 3 5 7 9 8 6 4 2

Library of Congress Cataloging-in-Publication Data
Amdur, Richard.
   Wilderness Preservation/by Richard Amdur: introduction by
   Russell E. Train.
      p. cm.—(Earth at risk)
   Includes bibliographical references and index.
   Summary: Discusses the degradation or destruction of
remaining wilderness areas on the Earth and possible ways to
save them.
   ISBN 0-7910-1580-7
         0-7910-1605-6 (pbk.)
   1. Nature conservation—Juvenile literature. 2. Wilderness
areas—Juvenile literature. 3. Rain forest conservation—Juvenile
literature. [1. Wilderness areas. 2. Conservation of natural
resources. 3. Environmental protection.]
I. Title. II. Series.   92-10594
QH75.A49 1993   CIP
333.76′137—dc20   AC

C O N T E N T S

INTRODUCTION

Russell E. Train

Administrator, Environmental Protection Agency, 1973 to 1977; Chairman of the Board of Directors, World Wildlife Fund and the Conservation Foundation

There is a growing realization that human activities increasingly are threatening the health of the natural systems that make life possible on this planet. Humankind has the power to alter nature fundamentally, perhaps irreversibly.

This stark reality was dramatized in January 1989 when *Time* magazine named Earth the "Planet of the Year." In the same year, the Exxon *Valdez* disaster sparked public concern over the effects of human activity on vulnerable ecosystems when a thick blanket of crude oil coated the shores and wildlife of Prince William Sound in Alaska. And, no doubt, the 20th anniversary celebration of Earth Day in April 1990 renewed broad public interest in environmental issues still further. It is no accident then that many people are calling the years between 1990 and 2000 the "Decade of the Environment."

And this is not merely a case of media hype, for the 1990s will truly be a time when the people of the planet Earth learn the meaning of the phrase "everything is connected to everything else" in the natural and man-made systems that sustain our lives. This will be a period when more people will understand that burning a tree in Amazonia adversely affects the global atmosphere just as much as the exhaust from the cars that fill our streets and expressways.

Central to our understanding of environmental issues is the need to recognize the complexity of the problems we face and the relationships between environmental and other needs in our society. Global warming provides an instructive example. Controlling emissions of carbon dioxide, the principal greenhouse gas, will involve efforts to reduce the use of fossil fuels to generate electricity. Such a reduction will include energy conservation and the promotion of alternative energy sources, such as nuclear and solar power.

The automobile contributes significantly to the problem. We have the choice of switching to more energy-efficient autos and, in the longer run, of choosing alternative automotive power systems and relying more on mass transit. This will require different patterns of land use and development, patterns that are less transportation and energy intensive.

In agriculture, rice paddies and cattle are major sources of greenhouse gases. Recent experiments suggest that universally used nitrogen fertilizers may inhibit the ability of natural soil organisms to take up methane, thus contributing tremendously to the atmospheric loading of that gas—one of the major culprits in the global warming scenario.

As one explores the various parameters of today's pressing environmental challenges, it is possible to identify some areas where we have made some progress. We have taken important steps to control gross pollution over the past two decades. What I find particularly encouraging is the growing environmental consciousness and activism by today's youth. In many communities across the country, young people are working together to take their environmental awareness out of the classroom and apply it to everyday problems. Successful recycling and tree-planting projects have been launched as a result of these budding environmentalists who have committed themselves to a cleaner environment. Citizen action, activated by youthful enthusiasm, was largely responsible for the fast-food industry's switch from rainforest to domestic beef, for pledges from important companies in the tuna industry to use fishing techniques that would not harm dolphins, and for the recent announcement by the McDonald's Corporation to phase out polystyrene "clam shell" hamburger containers.

Despite these successes, much remains to be done if we are to make ours a truly healthy environment. Even a short list of persistent issues includes problems such as acid rain, ground-level ozone and smog, and airborne toxins; groundwater protection and nonpoint sources of pollution, such as runoff from farms and city streets; wetlands protection; hazardous waste dumps; and solid waste disposal, waste minimization, and recycling.

Similarly, there is an unfinished agenda in the natural resources area: effective implementation of newly adopted management plans for national forests; strengthening the wildlife refuge system; national park management, including addressing the growing pressure of development on lands surrounding the parks; implementation of the Endangered Species Act; wildlife trade problems, such as that involving elephant ivory; and ensuring adequate sustained funding for these efforts at all levels of government. All of these issues are before us today; most will continue in one form or another through the year 2000.

Each of these challenges to environmental quality and our health requires a response that recognizes the complex nature of the problem. Narrowly conceived solutions will not achieve lasting results. Often it seems that when we grab hold of one part of the environmental balloon, an unsightly and threatening bulge appears somewhere else.

The higher environmental issues arise on the national agenda, the more important it is that we are armed with the best possible knowledge of the economic costs of undertaking particular environmental programs and the costs associated with not undertaking them. Our society is not blessed with unlimited resources, and tough choices are going to have to be made. These should be informed choices.

All too often, environmental objectives are seen as at cross-purposes with other considerations vital to our society. Thus, environmental protection is often viewed as being in conflict with economic growth, with energy needs, with agricultural productions, and so on. The time has come when environmental considerations must be fully integrated into every nation's priorities.

One area that merits full legislative attention is energy efficiency. The United States is one of the least energy efficient of all the industrialized nations. Japan, for example, uses far less energy per unit of gross national product than the United States does. Of course, a country as large as the United States requires large amounts of energy for transportation. However, there is still a substantial amount of excess energy used, and this excess constitutes waste. More fuel-efficient autos and home heating systems would save millions of barrels of oil, or their equivalent, each year. And air pollutants, including greenhouse gases, could be significantly reduced by increased efficiency in industry.

I suspect that the environmental problem that comes closest to home for most of us is the problem of what to do with trash. All over the world, communities are wrestling with the problem of waste disposal. Landfill sites are rapidly filling to capacity. No one wants a trash and garbage dump near home. As William Ruckelshaus, former EPA administrator and now in the waste management business, puts it, "Everyone wants you to pick up the garbage and no one wants you to put it down!"

At the present time, solid waste programs emphasize the regulation of disposal, setting standards for landfills, and so forth. In the decade ahead, we must shift our emphasis from regulating waste disposal to an overall reduction in its volume. We must look at the entire waste stream, including product design and packaging. We must avoid creating waste in the first place. To the greatest extent possible, we should then recycle any waste that is produced. I believe that, while most of us enjoy our comfortable way of life and have no desire to change things, we also know in our hearts that our "disposable society" has allowed us to become pretty soft.

Land use is another domestic issue that might well attract legislative attention by the year 2000. All across the United States, communities are grappling with the problem of growth. All too often, growth imposes high costs on the environment—the pollution of aquifers; the destruction of wetlands; the crowding of shorelines; the loss of wildlife habitat; and the loss of those special places, such as a historic structure or area, that give a community a sense of identity. It is worth noting that growth is not only the product of economic development but of population movement. By the year 2010, for example, experts predict that 75% of all Americans will live within 50 miles of a coast.

It is important to keep in mind that we are all made vulnerable by environmental problems that cross international borders. Of course, the most critical global conservation problems are the destruction of tropical forests and the consequent loss of their biological capital. Some scientists have calculated extinction rates as high as 11 species per hour. All agree that the loss of species has never been greater than at the present time; not even the disappearance of the dinosaurs can compare to today's rate of extinction.

In addition to species extinctions, the loss of tropical forests may represent as much as 20% of the total carbon dioxide loadings to the atmosphere. Clearly, any international approach to the problem of global warming must include major efforts to stop the destruction of forests and to manage those that remain on a renewable basis. Debt for nature swaps, which the World Wildlife Fund has pioneered in Costa Rica, Ecuador, Madagascar, and the Philippines, provide a useful mechanism for promoting such conservation objectives.

Global environmental issues inevitably will become the principal focus in international relations. But the single overriding issue facing the world community today is how to achieve a sustainable balance between growing human populations and the earth's natural systems. If you travel as frequently as I do in the developing countries of Latin America, Africa, and Asia, it is hard to escape the reality that expanding human populations are seriously weakening the earth's resource base. Rampant deforestation, eroding soils, spreading deserts, loss of biological diversity, the destruction of fisheries, and polluted and degraded urban environments threaten to spread environmental impoverishment, particularly in the tropics, where human population growth is greatest.

It is important to recognize that environmental degradation and human poverty are closely linked. Impoverished people desperate for land on which to grow crops or graze cattle are destroying forests and overgrazing even more marginal land. These people become trapped in a vicious downward spiral. They have little choice but to continue to overexploit the weakened resources available to them. Continued abuse of these lands only diminishes their productivity. Throughout the developing world, alarming amounts of land rendered useless by over-grazing and poor agricultural practices have become virtual wastelands, yet human numbers continue to multiply in these areas.

From Bangladesh to Haiti, we are confronted with an increasing number of ecological basket cases. In the Philippines, a traditional focus of U.S. interest, environmental devastation is widespread as defores-tation, soil erosion, and the destruction of coral reefs and fisheries combine with the highest population growth rate in Southeast Asia.

Controlling human population growth is the key factor in the environmental equation. World population is expected to at least double to about 11 billion before leveling off. Most of this growth will occur in the poorest nations of the developing world. I would hope that the United States will once again become a strong advocate of international efforts to promote family planning. Bringing human populations into a sustainable balance with their natural resource base must be a vital objective of U.S. foreign policy.

Foreign economic assistance, the program of the Agency for International Development (AID), can become a potentially powerful tool for arresting environmental deterioration in developing countries. People who profess to care about global environmental problems— the loss of biological diversity, the destruction of tropical forests, the greenhouse effect, the impoverishment of the marine environment, and so on—should be strong supporters of foreign aid planning and the principles of sustainable development urged by the World Commission on Environment and Development, the "Brundtland Commission."

If sustainability is to be the underlying element of overseas assistance programs, so too must it be a guiding principle in people's practices at home. Too often we think of sustainable development only in terms of the resources of other countries. We have much that we can and should be doing to promote long-term sustainability in our own resource management. The conflict over our own rainforests, the old growth forests of the Pacific Northwest, illustrates this point.

The decade ahead will be a time of great activity on the environmental front, both globally and domestically. I sincerely believe we will be tested as we have been only in times of war and during the Great Depression. We must set goals for the year 2000 that will challenge both the American people and the world community.

Despite the complexities ahead, I remain an optimist. I am confident that if we collectively commit ourselves to a clean, healthy environment we can surpass the achievements of the 1980s and meet the serious challenges that face us in the coming decades. I hope that today's students will recognize their significant role in and responsibility for bringing about change and will rise to the occasion to improve the quality of our global environment.

The Grand Canyon National Park, one of the most spectacular natural areas in the United States.

chapter 1

THE VANISHING WILDERNESS

On a 1.5 million-acre strip of land fronting the Arctic Ocean along the northern coast of Alaska, a fabulous wildlife spectacle is almost always on display. Polar bears, musk oxen, Dall sheep, wolverines, and millions of waterfowl are just some of the animal species that cavort, feed, and mate in the area. Nearly 200,000 caribou migrate here every spring in order to calve. The natural beauty, too, is compelling, from the forests and peaks of the Brooks Range to glacier-fed rivers and the broad, wildflower-speckled tundra. This is Alaska's Arctic National Wildlife Refuge, created in 1980 by an act of Congress aimed at preserving one of America's greatest natural areas. Save for some Native Americans and the occasional visitor, humans are nowhere to be seen.

Conservationists want to keep it that way. They have been pressing to have the region designated as a protected wilderness area. But geologists say there is a chance that large oil deposits lie beneath the coastal plain. Given the nation's thirst for new, reliable sources of oil, an effort was begun to open the area to oil industry exploration, sparking one of the greatest land disputes of the 1980s and 1990s. The proposal for exploratory drilling continues to be backed by the oil companies, the state of Alaska, the state's congressional delegation, and the administration of President George Bush. Opponents contest the scientific findings and fear irreparable harm to the native peoples and wildlife—and to the ecosystem in general—if development is allowed. Ironically, it took an environmental disaster in another part of the state—the 1989 Exxon *Valdez* oil spill—to bring all pending congressional legislation covering the area to a dead stop, at least temporarily. However, the battle is far from over. The fear over uncertain supplies of foreign oil that accompanied the Persian Gulf war has accelerated efforts by the Bush administration to open the refuge to oil companies.

The conflict underscores a truth about the way Americans feel about the country's fabled wilderness areas and national parks: They love them. So do the millions of tourists from around the world who come to the United States solely to experience its breathtaking natural beauty. They love photographing Half Dome in California's stunning Yosemite Valley. They love watching the more or less hourly eruptions of Yellowstone National Park's Old Faithful geyser. They love camping in the beautiful forests and hiking in the remote, open countryside. Unfortunately, they may be loving America's wilderness to death.

For one thing, there may be no such thing anymore as "getting away from it all." Visits to national parks are projected to surpass 600 million people per year by 2010, up from 33 million in 1950 and 300 million in the mid-1980s. Encounters with the great outdoors are looking more and more like standing-room-only sporting events—or the Indy 500, considering the booming popularity of off-road vehicles such as Jeeps, four-wheel-drive trucks, and heavy-duty mountain bikes. Not surprisingly, traffic jams have also increased. A major entrance to Yosemite National Park, which was clogged well beyond capacity, had to be closed one holiday weekend. Other problems commonly associated with day-to-day city life are showing up in the wilderness. Pollution at the Grand Canyon in Arizona often creates a haze so thick it is difficult to make out the opposite rim.

Logging and road building. Oil exploration. Strip mining. Development for tourism and recreation. These are just some of the many threats facing the nation's wilderness areas, from

Logging is one of the greatest threats to the wilderness, but the nation's demand for wood and wood products continues to grow, and thousands of jobs would be lost if the timber industry were more closely regulated.

Maine's Moosehorn National Wildlife Refuge to Florida's
Everglades and the southern California desert. The campaign
to preserve this vanishing wilderness is being fought on several
fronts—in Congress, in the courts, in factories and boardrooms,
and even in the nation's homes.

A   GLOBAL   CRISIS

The problem is by no means confined to the United
States. In Canada, for example, miners and real estate developers
want access to the Lake Timagami wilderness region in northern
Ontario. Logging has already begun there, and Canadian conservationists want their government to designate more of the
region as officially protected wilderness. Acid rain has killed 400
lakes and threatens over 40,000 more in Ontario alone. It has also
damaged countless trees all along the U.S.-Canada border. Many
Canadians claim this acid rain is caused by factory emissions in
the United States, a point of considerable tension between the
two nations.

Other wilderness areas and forests, especially rainforests,
in South America, central Africa, and Southeast Asia are being
devastated at the alarming rate of between 50 and 100 acres per
minute. This is done in great part to meet the demand of the industrialized nations for beef. To raise cattle, land must be cleared
for grazing. Industrialized countries, especially Japan, also have
an appetite for furniture made of hardwoods such as teak, mahog-
any, and ebony, causing still more stands of trees to fall.

Deforestation in Nepal takes a more localized form.
Population growth in this poor, tiny country nestled in the Hima-
layas between China and India is outpacing its ability to feed and

fuel itself. The result? Nepalis clear forests on their own to obtain wood for cooking and heating fires. They also clear land, through a technique known as slash-and-burn clearing, higher and higher up the sides of mountains to create more and more terraces of tillable soil. This in turn hastens topsoil erosion on hills already prone to it. Once lost, topsoil is gone forever.

Similar situations confront virtually every country in the world in one form or another. Madagascar, the island nation off the coast of East Africa, has lost 93% of its tropical forests. Ethiopia has lost 90%. More than a quarter of the African continent has turned into desert, with floods and famine the ongoing results. In Central America, experts say that all the rainforests outside protected areas could disappear within the next few decades. Irian Jaya, the Indonesian half of the island of New Guinea, is almost completely covered with forests, coral reefs, mangrove swamps, and savannah grasslands. All of this, however, is under increasing threat from logging, mining, the demand for agricultural land, and government plans to resettle people away from the archipelago's more crowded islands.

It is no exaggeration to call the current situation an emergency. With it has come an urgent need to respond to a number of vexing questions, among them: How much wilderness should be preserved as is? How much wilderness should be exploited for its natural resources? How much wilderness should be set aside for exploitation by future generations? Should wilderness be off-limits to tourists and vacationers?

What is the proper role of government in managing wilderness areas? How does anyone "manage" the wilderness? What happens when the desire to preserve wilderness comes into competition with peoples' jobs and survival? Men and women in

Deforestation in Haiti. This woman is desperately searching for scrap wood, the only fuel available for cooking.

the United States work as loggers to feed and house their families. Peasant villagers in India fell trees for much the same reasons, although in different ways. What other options do they have?

Who pays for wilderness preservation? In the United States, federal funding for the purchase of park land was nearly eliminated—cut from $681 million in 1978 to just $17 million—in 1989. Countries facing some of the most dire environmental predicaments are also some of the world's poorest and face a variety of daunting economic problems. What criteria should be used in setting their spending priorities?

The vanishing wilderness is a truly global crisis. With the wilderness so clearly in decline, scientists have said that human civilization could collapse in the foreseeable future. The wilderness is not something separate from humanity. It represents the biological foundation of human activity. It is a source of useful and renewable materials, and it moderates the climate. It is an integral part of processes that cycle and recyle energy, water, chemicals, and gases essential to life. To tame the wilderness, to overexploit it, to destroy it, is to gamble that industry and technology can solve all problems—that it is possible to survive in a totally artificial world of people's own making. If that gamble proves to be a foolish one, we may not realize it until it is too late.

John Muir and friend in Yosemite National Park. Muir, a nature writer and conservationist, founded the Sierra Club in 1892.

chapter 2

WHY PRESERVE WILDERNESS?

Wilderness is generally thought of, and is defined by most dictionaries, as an area or a region of land that is uncultivated and uninhabited by human beings. This is accurate enough, but the idea of wilderness, at least as understood by Americans, has always implied a good deal more and has undergone considerable evolution since the first settlers arrived in this country from Europe nearly 500 years ago.

The early settlers regarded the wilderness as something to be feared. They were plagued by nightmare visions of predatory wild animals and also feared the Native Americans with whom they came into violent contact. As historian and wilderness expert Roderick Nash wrote in *Wilderness and the American Mind:* "Safety and comfort, even necessities like food and shelter, depended on overcoming the wild environment. For the first Americans, as for medieval Europeans, the forest's darkness hid savage men, wild beasts, and still stranger creatures of the imagination." Everything in the New World was defined in terms of the needs of the colonizers. The word *wilderness* defined land that was considered useless. The environment either provided the materials necessary for survival or it was considered wasteland, and one was free to transform it into something useful and productive for human beings.

The idea of making a new start in a new land was powerful enough to allay the worst of the settlers' fears. Over time, the success they achieved became total. Imbued with the "frontier spirit," they moved west across the United States, driving out foreign powers and conquering the Indians. Enormous gains in technology and industry brought about the rapid growth of cities and the spread of agriculture, enabling Americans to claim that they had "tamed" the very wilderness that had earlier filled them with dread.

The first settlers found support for this kind of thinking— that humans should dominate nature—in the Bible. It is written in Genesis that human beings should "be fruitful, and multiply, and replenish the earth, and subdue it; and have dominion over the fish of the sea, and over the fowl of the air, and over every living thing that creepeth upon the earth." American settlers can be partially forgiven for taking this command to heart. They felt they had a God-given right to use the wilderness as they saw fit. The land was ready to be conquered, transformed, and put to human use.

The land itself was something of a paradise. The soil was as rich and fertile as any they had ever run through their fingers. The rivers teemed with fish. The mountains were covered with beautiful forests, and the ground was rich with mineral ores. Most people never would have dreamed that such things could grow scarce in a land of unparalleled plenty. The American land seemed a place of unlimited bounty that could be exploited without consequence. Many generations of Americans acted on this thinking. But as they settled the continent, a horrible toll was exacted upon forests and wildlands. The woods of New England, the Great Lakes region, California, and the Pacific Northwest were cut down. The Appalachians were gouged with coal mines. The huge prairies of the Midwest came under cultivation. Railroads crossed the southwestern deserts. Wildlife retreated or died. Pollution became a new fact of life.

This pattern is rapidly being repeated throughout the world in countries that are still developing. These countries find that to overcome their backwardness they are under great pressure to exploit the resources of their wilderness areas. Exploitation of forests, grazing lands, wetlands and coastal areas, and unique natural habitats—and the commercial products taken from these ecosystems—may be all that some nations have to finance their development.

To speak of wilderness today is to speak not of vast areas of unspoiled countryside but of small, remote parks and reserves hemmed in from all sides by developed communities. Now, to see wilderness, people must often travel hundreds of miles and pay fees to enter national parks. And yet, as the extent of wilderness has contracted, people's desires to experience it have increased.

There are a number of compelling scientific, economic, and ecological reasons for preserving the wilderness. In a nutshell, say experts, the planet's well-being depends on it. Natural ecosystems have been moderating and stabilizing the earth's environment—and making it suitable for human habitation—long before people came to depend on industrial technology to make their lives more comfortable. Even the relatively small areas of wilderness that remain are vitally important to human communities.

First of all, wilderness areas protect watersheds. Watersheds are large areas of land, often in the form of large valleys or broad plains surrounded by mountains or highlands, from which rainwater drains from brooks and streams into major river systems. The British call such areas catchments, and this is accurate in that such geographical areas are essential for the recapturing and channeling of the fresh water upon which both cities and rural communities depend. Water is probably the single most valuable of the earth's natural resources. All forms of life—plant, animal, and human—would perish without it. People need water for drinking, washing, cooking, cleaning, farming, fighting fires, generating electricity, and more. Watersheds not only gather water; they regulate its supply. The forests and plant ecosystems in these drainage basins act like sponges, holding enough water to prevent floods and releasing it slowly and consistently over time, which prevents droughts. Forest cover, in effect, slows down the global water cycle, giving other living creatures time to make use of this resource before rivers carry the water back to the sea.

Where the supply of water has been deemed insufficient, that is, where human communities have been allowed to grow so large that natural watersheds cannot supply them, human beings have intervened and tried to ensure their water supply by building dams at strategic points along rivers or streams. Dams trap water, creating reservoirs that enable the flow of water to be increased as needed. Dams can also be used to tap the energy of moving water to provide hydroelectric power. There is a price to pay, however.

Reservoirs sometimes flood and destroy areas of wilderness behind the dam. The migratory patterns of certain fish are disrupted, possibly leading to their extinction. The deposition of silt and organic materials ceases, thus affecting the fertility of land downstream and decreasing agricultural productivity. The hydroelectric turbines themselves may become fouled by silt, and silt will certainly build up in the reservoirs, shallowing them over time, thereby reducing water pressure and electric power output. Dams are an attempt to outdo the efficiency and usefulness of natural watersheds, and the evidence coming to light is showing that this tampering with natural systems is proving to be more costly and problematic than anyone imagined.

To function properly, watersheds need to be protected against soil runoff, which means preserving the vegetative cover that keeps the soil in place. This will not be possible, environmentalists believe, if these areas are opened to logging and mining interests and other forms of commercial development.

Wilderness areas serve as critical wildlife habitats. The building of roads, dams, farms, and homes on formerly empty land has changed age-old animal migratory, mating, and feeding patterns. It will do the migratory birds of the Amazon little good to save the rainforests if their northern habitats in the forests and wetlands of the United States and Canada are destroyed. Elephants, wolves, grizzly bears, mountain lions, gorillas, and many other animals have been brought to the brink of extinction. If only a few species disappear, civilization will probably not stop to notice. But there is the danger of tipping the delicate balance and destroying the intricate biological webs that support human life in ways not yet clearly understood by scientists.

Conservationists have also raised the ethical issue of whether or not other species have the right to exist even if they seem to serve no useful purpose to people.

The issue of preserving species is a complex one. Biologists and ecologists have introduced a new term—biodiversity—to try to make people understand that the existence of many different kinds of organisms is in itself a valuable thing. Wilderness areas preserve the biological diversity of life. Humans may be the most sophisticated and advanced species on earth, but they are connected to all others, whether they like it or not. More and more people have come to accept that the survival of the human species could very well depend on the survival of other species. In 1986, nine prominent biologists, members of the U.S. National Academy of Science, said, "The species extinction crisis is a threat to civilization second only to the threat of thermonuclear war."

The value of biodiversity comes home to people in the fields of scientific and medical research. Plant and animal species found in the wilderness, existing in their natural states, have been used to develop antibiotics and medicines used to treat cancer,

The northern spotted owl, also a resident of the old-growth forests of the Pacific Northwest. Efforts to protect these forests and save the owl's habitat have angered local loggers.

heart disease, and many other conditions. Indeed, more than 25% of all the prescriptions sold in the United States each year—with a value of some $10 billion—contain active ingredients from plants. Researchers are only beginning to tap the wilderness for its unique and irreplaceable riches. The issue goes far beyond new medicines. Maintaining genetic variety in food plants has helped farmers increase crop yields and enabled them to produce harvests under adverse environmental conditions.

An example of the problems created by obtaining new medicines from nature is shown in the case of taxol, a new cancer drug derived from the bark of the Pacific yew tree. Dr. Samuel Broder, director of the National Cancer Institute, told the *New York Times* in May 1991 that taxol is "the most important new drug we have had in cancer for fifteen years. I'm not saying it's a cure, but I will tell you there are women who failed every other treatment who responded." One study reported that taxol was "extraordinarily effective" against advanced breast cancer. Not surprisingly, demand for the drug is expected to grow dramatically.

But to make enough taxol to treat one cancer patient requires six 100-year-old yew trees. The trees are also extremely difficult to harvest. They grow not in groves but in isolation throughout the Pacific Northwest. Even if they could be located and reached, logging is prohibited on much of this land to protect the habitat of the northern spotted owl. Even if they could be logged, most of the trees are too small to be used.

No one knows for certain how many Pacific yews there are, since no inventory has ever been done by the U.S. Forest Service and the Bureau of Land Management, the government agencies that preside over the land. In fact, for years the trees were considered so commercially unimportant that many were treated no better than weeds—cut down and burned as part of logging operations designed to harvest other trees. If the yews are to be harvested to make taxol, conservationists want to be sure enough remain as a source for the future. Somewhat defusing the controversy is scientists' acknowledgment that, given the yew tree's scarcity, the future of taxol as an accessible treatment option lies in the ability to synthesize it.

Wilderness areas also control and moderate climate and help to recycle gases essential to human life. Through the process of photosynthesis, green plants and trees take carbon dioxide present in the atmosphere and turn it into the oxygen humans need for respiration. Trees thereby cleanse the atmosphere of excess carbon that is at the root of global warming, the buildup of CO_2 and other gases that retain heat and threaten to increase the planet's overall temperature. This climate change, which some experts say has already begun to occur, has several potentially dangerous consequences: the flooding of heavily populated coastal areas because of the melting of the polar ice caps, increased desertification, widespread crop failures, and unpredictable rainfall patterns. Reversing the process is now one of the environmental movement's highest priorities.

Sometimes the value of wilderness areas conflicts with its use. Wilderness areas offer opportunities for outdoor recreation and serve as havens from the pressures of modern life. Americans are taking to the outdoors in ever-increasing numbers, sparking a boom in the tourist and outdoor-gear industries. Wilderness areas, under properly managed conditions, serve as places for hiking, horseback riding, hunting, fishing, bird watching, mountain climbing, canoeing, and camping—all amid magnificent natural beauty. But this very appreciation of the wilderness, if overused, can destroy it.

Wilderness areas benefit humans in ways they do not yet understand. As a spokesperson for the National Audubon Society once said, the wilderness has "answers to questions we haven't learned how to ask yet." In this sense, the wilderness retains some of the mystery it had for early American settlers. Wilderness areas satisfy spiritual needs. Many prominent Americans have revealed deep, worshipful feelings about the importance of the wilderness. Former Supreme Court justice William O. Douglas wrote that the wilderness helped preserve the "capacity for wonder—the power to feel, if not see, the miracles of life, of beauty, and of harmony around us." John Muir, one of the nation's earliest and most influential conservationists—the popular Muir Woods, which are north of San Francisco, California, are named after him—called the wilderness "the hope of the world." Henry David Thoreau, the writer, philosopher, and naturalist, wrote in his 1861 essay "Walking" what are perhaps the most frequently quoted words about the wilderness: "The West of which I speak is but another name for the Wild, and what I have been preparing to say is, that in Wildness is the preservation of the World."

The bark of Taxus brevifolia, the yew tree, contains a rare chemical that is used to fight certain kinds of cancer, but the tree is rapidly disappearing as the old-growth forests of the Pacific Northwest are destroyed.

Forests help to regulate the flow of water through the hydrologic cycle, absorbing rainfall and releasing it slowly and steadily. When forests disappear, there is an increase in floods and droughts.

chapter 3

WHERE IS THE WILDERNESS?

In the late 1980s, researchers for the Sierra Club spent roughly 18 months examining aerial navigation charts created by the U.S. Defense Mapping Agency. The Sierra Club, one of the country's leading environmental organizations, was interested in finding those areas of the country completely free of landmarks. Ignoring anything that looked like a road, a reservoir, or an oil well, they searched for tracts of land consisting of at least 1 million acres that bore no sign of human habitation or alteration. Their goal was to make an accurate tally of the world's wilderness. Given the facts of worldwide deforestation and the spread of humanity across the globe, they wanted to answer a simple question: How much was left?

Their findings, reported in *Ambio* and *Science News*, indicated that one-third of the earth's landmass—over 18 million square miles—remains wild. Generally, those areas exist in several broad swaths. One stretches across the northernmost part of the former Soviet Union into northern Alaska and Canada. Another runs southwest from the far eastern part of the former Soviet Union through Tibet and Afghanistan, across the Arabian peninsula and into Africa's Great Rift valley. A third takes the form of an east-west belt across Africa's Sahara Desert. The fourth runs north-south through the center of Australia. Only relatively small patches of wilderness were seen in those areas traditionally thought to be undisturbed, in Africa, in the Amazon basin, and in areas along the Andes range in South America. Of these remaining wildlands, about 30% is forest, and 70% is tundra and desert too hot, too cold, or too dry for cultivation or development.

When wilderness is calculated as a percentage of total land area for each continent, the list is as follows: Antarctica, 100% wilderness; North America, 36%; Africa, 30%; Oceania (Australia, New Zealand, and the Pacific islands), 30%; Asia, 27%; South America, 20%; and Europe, 7%. When the percentage of wilderness is calculated for specific countries, the list is as follows: Greenland, 99% wilderness; Canada, 65%; Algeria, 64%; Egypt, 47%; the former Soviet Union, 39%; Australia, 33%; Brazil, 28%; China, 19%; and the United States, only 3.9%. One alarming fact emerged from the Sierra Club survey: less than 20% of the identified wilderness in the world is legally protected from exploitation.

THE NATIONAL WILDERNESS PRESERVATION SYSTEM

In the United States, there are approximately 90.7 million acres of federally protected wilderness. This represents a little less than 4% of the United States's 2.2 billion acres of land. There are some 474 distinct wilderness areas—43 in Alaska and 431 in the rest of the country. Every state has at least one wilderness preserve except Connecticut, Delaware, Iowa, Kansas, Maryland, and Rhode Island. Well over half of this total wild- erness area—56.5 million acres—is in Alaska, including the nation's largest wilderness area, an 8.7-million-acre expanse located in Wrangell–Saint Elias National Park.

That the acreage of Alaska's Wrangell–Saint Elias National Park is greater than any other state's total wilderness area highlights an important fact: only 1.8% of the land in the lower 48 states has been preserved as wilderness. Most of that—about one-third of the total wilderness system—is in the 11 states of the American West: Arizona, California, Colorado, Idaho, Montana, Nevada, New Mexico, Oregon, Utah, Wash- ington, and Wyoming. After Alaska, California has the most wilderness. The largest single wilderness area in the lower 48 states, totaling 2.3 million acres, is Idaho's Frank Church–River of No Return Wilderness Preserve.

Only 4.7% of the wilderness lands are in the eastern half of the United States. Almost half of this land can be found in just two areas: Florida's Everglades National Park—the second largest wilderness area in the lower 48 states—and Minnesota's Boundary Waters Canoe Area. Florida, incidentally, also boasts the nation's smallest wliderness area, the six-acre Pelican Island National Wildlife Refuge. The northeastern United States has the smallest amount of wilderness. In the 11 states from Maryland to Maine, home to nearly 25% of the nation's population, there are only 192,686 acres of wilderness, just two-tenths of one percent of the total wilderness area and less than two-hundredths of one percent of the land area of the northeastern states.

There is no single government agency charged with the responsibility of preserving all the nation's wilderness. Rather, the power to administer wilderness areas is splintered among a number of different federal agencies with different mandates and goals. As government land management practices in the United States have evolved over the years, these various agencies often work at cross-purposes trying to enforce laws whose aims are sometimes contradictory. As a result, part of the battle being fought by conservationists is not simply for wilderness preservation but for a sensible and coordinated government policy toward protected lands. The issue is extremely important to conservationists and many others as well, because federal public lands, which also include categories other than wilderness areas, amount to more than 600 million acres—more than 25% of America's entire land base.

THE CLASSIFICATION OF WILDERNESS AREAS

Roughly 42.5% of America's protected wilderness areas—38.5 million acres—are part of the National Park System. Currently, there are 339 national parks and monuments totaling roughly 80 million acres. The National Park Service was created in 1916 as part of the Department of the Interior to administer the country's growing number of parks. As the original legislation creating the Park Service stated, its mission was "to conserve the scenery and the natural and historic objects and wildlife therein and to provide for the enjoyment of the same in such manner and by such means as will leave them unimpaired for the enjoyment of future generations." The intention of the legislation was that the land was to be strictly preserved, kept off-limits to logging, mining, and road building unless special dispensation

Millions of wildfowl depend upon undisturbed wetlands for nourishment and rest as they migrate along their flyways. As these lands are filled in and turned into residential developments, the birds will disappear.

was granted by Congress. The grazing of cattle and livestock is permitted if the activity was well established on the land before its designation as a national park.

In practice, however, America's national parks, and therefore the wilderness areas within them, face a variety of threats. The Park Service itself, during and especially following World War II, shifted from its original preservation ethic toward one of managed use. Seeking to exploit the park's wealth of natural resources, the Service encouraged commercial logging and mining. Tourism was also promoted to such a degree that, in the eyes of most observers, it has now reached unmanageable proportions.

It has also become clear in recent years that the ecosystems of which the parks are a part do not simply end at the park borders. Pollution, for example, does not respect human-made boundaries. Development on unprotected lands adjacent to the parks is a problem of growing magnitude.

Another 35.7% of American wilderness—32.4 million acres—is found within the National Forest System, administered by the National Forest Service, an agency of the Department of Agriculture. The Forest Service controls 123 forest areas encompassing 191 million acres of land. It was created in 1905 to halt the unregulated abuse of federal forestland, which had been the norm for generations as the country grew. As Dyan Zaslowsky reports in *These American Lands*, "In its scope, in the amount of wood taken, and in the swiftness of its passage, there was nothing in human history to compare with the decades of this astonishing assault on the natural world. And there was precious little done to stop it." President Theodore Roosevelt, a renowned outdoorsman and early conservationist, declared at the time of the Forest Service's creation, "In the past we have admitted the right of the individual to injure the future of the Republic for his present profit. The time has come for a change."

As originally conceived, the national forestlands and the wilderness areas within them were supposed to be managed and protected following the principle of "multiple use," which attempts to achieve a compromise between preservation and economic growth. In 1905, then Secretary of Agriculture James Wilson wrote: "Where conflicting interests must be reconciled the question will always be decided from the standpoint of the greatest good of the greatest number in the long run."

Multiple use was and remains a controversial idea and has given rise to hundreds of conflicts between conservationists and developers over the years. Extensive timber harvesting, road building, camping, and tourist activities have been permitted on national forestlands, all under the direction of the Forest Service. The tipping of the scales toward "use" accelerated following World War II. Timber was needed not just in the United States but also in Europe to help rebuild after the devastation of the war. To get at this timber, roads were needed. Thus began the assault on national forestlands that continues to this day. Protection of the forests has, according to most conservationists, received a very low priority from the National Forest Service, not at all in keeping with the spirit of multiple use.

Another 21.3%—19.3 million acres—of American wilderness is part of the National Wildlife Refuge System. More than half of the roughly 4,500 species of mammals, fish, and birds native to the United States—including 75 endangered species—

Wetlands also provide people with areas for recreational activities such as boating and fishing.

find the vital habitats they need in the 436 nature reserves that are part of this system. The federal government was relatively slow to extend its protection to the nation's wildlife. For many years that power was left to the individual states as a debate raged over who owned the wildlife. As fur trapping depleted the beaver population, as bird breeding grounds were plowed under for fields, and as wetlands were filled in by expanding cities, the need for a cohesive national policy became clear. In 1940, the Fish and Wildlife Service was created by combining the Bureau of Fisheries in the Department of Commerce with the Bureau of Biological Survey in the Department of Agriculture. The new agency became part of the Department of the Interior.

Unfortunately, the Fish and Wildlife Service, in the opinion of conservationists, lacks a clearly stated operating mandate. It has responsibilities beyond protecting and managing the country's wildlife refuges. Its power is also often challenged by state legislation that creates individual wildlife refuges operating under rules at odds with federal goals. The system is thus considered highly vulnerable to abuse. Indeed, government officials have allowed logging, grazing, energy exploration, and recreational development within national wildlife refuges.

A small number of American wilderness areas, less than 1% of the total—some 500,000 acres—is under the jurisdiction of the Bureau of Land Management (BLM). They are known as National Resource Lands. According to the Wilderness Society, "BLM territory is what remained after the states, homesteaders, mining companies and railroads staked their claims, and after the federal government carved out its national parks, monuments, forests, and wildlife refuges. BLM land is thus the last that remains of the old West." Grazing is the predominant activity, followed by energy extraction.

As the federal government assumed control of these lands, it came into conflict with ranchers, farmers, miners, and others who had grown accustomed to using the land as they wished, paying no fees and seeking no one's permission. But the need for federal control had become clear, especially during the 1930s, as decades of overgrazing finally resulted in the famed dust bowls, the effects of which were felt far beyond the plains of the Midwest and Southwest. Winds blew the dust as far as the East Coast, causing drivers in New York to use their headlights at midday.

In 1946, the Bureau of Land Management was founded as part of the Department of the Interior. Like national forests, BLM lands and the wilderness within are supposed to be administered according to the multiple-use principle. But the BLM was founded with no protective mandate and very little money to spend on enforcement. The result is that almost anything goes: grazing, mining, hunting, and off-road vehicles.

Conservationists have targeted BLM lands as having the greatest potential for the creation of new wilderness areas. BLM land holdings are extensive, and Congress has instructed the agency to survey its lands to decide which should be re-ommended for formal wilderness designation. A heated political battle, however, is expected. The agency's traditional sympathies lie with developers and those who preach aggressive use of federal lands. More ominously, conservationists claim, the BLM's initial inventory of its lands has ignored large areas of potential wilderness.

A dust storm in Oklahoma in 1935. Severe soil erosion occurs when forests and vegetative cover are destroyed.

Many other government agencies are involved in the administration of the nation's wilderness. The departments of Defense, Energy, and Transportation, the Army Corps of Engineers, and the National Aeronautics and Space Administration (NASA) all control small parcels of wilderness. Other federal lands include Indian reservations and military properties. Finally, other agencies that do not own federal land or wilderness areas nonetheless often play a role in their proposed uses.

The Environmental Protection Agency (EPA) is probably the best known of these. Created in 1970 to ensure compliance with the nation's environmental legislation, it is the largest independent regulatory agency in the federal government. It is also one of the most controversial. It is continually criticized by corporations and businesses for stifling economic growth, whereas conservationists complain that it is not doing enough to protect the environment.

As threats to the environment and the wilderness grow more complicated and extensive, the disputes—bureaucratic, administrative, and political—between these agencies and departments will only delay efforts to preserve the wilderness and make it more difficult to develop a comprehensive policy of management.

Wood is a renewable resource, and sustainable logging at controlled rates would protect the forests. Clear-cutting and the use of heavy machinery, no matter how destructive, is cheaper for the timber companies.

chapter   4

THE   WILDERNESS
UNDER   ATTACK

Some of the threats to the wilderness have not changed much since they were first identified decades ago; they have simply grown more pressing and more intractable. Other threats are of more recent vintage and are the stuff of today's headlines. One of the biggest problems facing conservationists is society's need for wood. Forests not only serve as watersheds, wildlife habitats, and recyclers of the world's oxygen and carbon;   they also provide the timber used for construction and the wood used for fuel and paper pulp, medicines, and many other products.

There is no questioning the world's need for timber. According to *Living in the Environment* by G. Tyler Miller, one-half of the world's annual timber harvest is used for heating and cooking fires, mostly in the lesser developed countries of Africa and Asia. Another one-third is formed into lumber for the veneer, panels, plywood, hardboard, particleboard, and chipboard used in construction. The remaining one-sixth is converted to pulp that is used for paper products such as newspapers, magazines, books, stationery, and packaging for consumer goods. The U.S. Forest

Service projects a doubling in domestic demand for wood products by the year 2030.

The task of ensuring a steady supply of timber to meet this demand is considered extremely difficult for the simple reason that forests are not like other crops that can be planted and harvested annually. Though they are technically a renewable resource, trees require anywhere from 20 to 1,000 years to reach maturity. The challenge has given rise to the science of forest management, which employs two systems: even-aged management and uneven-aged management.

Even-aged management means that all the trees in a particular stand are kept at approximately the same size and the same age. All the trees are harvested at the same time, after which the entire area is replanted so that another stand of same-age trees can grow. This method appeals to growers because the near-assembly-line conditions mean that they can maximize their return on investment in a relatively short time.

The first step in creating an even-aged stand of trees is to clear an area so that seedlings can be planted. This is usually done in what are known as old-growth forests—"virgin" or previously uncut forests that contain large, old trees together with trees of different ages. The newly planted trees are like a "crop" that can be harvested all together. Usually they are all of one species, chosen for various qualities of the wood. Timber industry managers and some U.S. Forest Service administrators say that these "tree farms," through the use of genetic engineering and other techniques, produce higher-quality wood in less time than if nature had been allowed to follow its course.

As its name indicates, uneven-aged management involves trees of many different ages and sizes. These trees are permitted to grow and regenerate naturally, meaning that biological diversity is maintained and that multiple use of the forest is still possible. Overall, this method of management is more in keeping with the natural cycle of a forest. Growers harvest periodically and achieve a reasonable return on their investment. Costs are higher because the trees harvested at any one time must be cut and removed without damaging the rest of the forest.

The actual harvesting of trees is done using several different methods, depending on the type of tree, the terrain, the type of forest management system, and the aims of the grower or landowner. Generally speaking, there are two basic methods: selective cutting and clear-cutting. Selective cutting involves the harvesting of middle-aged or mature trees, singly or in small groups, in uneven-aged forests. It is used to reduce crowding, to encourage the growth of younger trees, and to maintain the variety of trees in a particular stand. This method is preferred by those who want to preserve biological diversity and the multiple-use character of a particular piece of forest. However, selective cutting is labor intensive and requires much planning and skill. It can also be quite costly, since roads and trails may have to be reopened from time to time over the years to grant access to the stands.

Shelterwood cutting is a variation on selective cutting and can be done in either even-aged or uneven-aged forests. It involves harvesting all mature trees through a series of cuts made over the course of about ten years. The first cut opens up the forest by removing mature trees and those that are dead, diseased, or otherwise undesirable. The second cut removes more mature trees, reducing crowding and allowing more light to reach young trees and seedlings. The third and final cut removes still more mature trees, creating room for the newer trees. Shelterwood cutting leaves a multiple-use forest but is also costly and requires a good deal of skill and planning.

By far the most common method of tree harvesting in the United States—accounting for nearly two-thirds of U.S. timber production—is clear-cutting. Clear-cutting means removing all trees in a single harvest to create a new, even-aged stand or tree farm. Reforestation, the action of renewing forest cover, can be accomplished naturally—since tree seeds are released by the action of the harvest—or artificially by planting seedlings. The seedlings may have been raised in a nursery to achieve a gen-etically superior species in terms of wood quality or disease resistance or a fast growth rate. Whole-tree harvesting is a more "thorough" variation of clear-cutting that is used to create pulp or wood chips as opposed to lumber. Whereas conventional clear-cutting leaves behind a field of unusable stumps, whole-tree harvesting employs a machine that cuts trees at ground level. Sometimes even the roots are taken in an attempt to increase the per-acre yield of wood material.

For the timber industries of the United States and Canada, the virtues of clear-cutting are clear. It increases the volume of timber harvest per acre, sometimes, in the case of whole-tree harvesting, by as much as 300%. Clear-cutting also cuts costs by requiring much less planning and skill and by reducing the amount of road building needed to reach additional stands of trees. It permits reforestation to be done with genetically superior seedlings, meaning that a second harvest, or a third or fourth, can be performed sooner than if loggers had to wait for nature.

However beneficial clear-cutting has been for the logging industry, it has been disastrous for American and Canadian forests. Clear-cutting produces large, bare, unnatural, scarlike patches of wounded forest that take decades, if not centuries, to regenerate. There is controversy over the seriousness of the logging industry's efforts to reforest. Often the time and money spent to put seedlings into the bare ground and protect them during their initial stages of growth is minimal. But the problems go much deeper.

When, as often happens, clear-cutting is performed on steep slopes, it causes soil erosion, siltation of streams and rivers from the runoff of ground sediment, flooding from heavy rains, and even landslides when the remaining tree roots rot away. This also depletes the soil of nutrients, lessening its biological productivity. Wildlife habitats are also damaged or destroyed, decreasing biological diversity. For example, clear-cutting done near some rivers has eliminated their natural shade, raising water temperatures to levels that have proved lethal to salmon and trout. Even the recreational value of the land is harmed. Hikers and campers seek spots where they can gaze upon vistas of natural beauty, not man-made eyesores.

THE CONSERVATIONIST'S COMPLAINT

But clear-cutting is just one aspect of the larger issue of the effects of commercial logging as currently practiced in the United States and Canada. Because politics and law are involved, and because jobs and money are at stake, the battle between conservationists and the timber industry has been passionate, to say the least.

Conservationists begin their criticism of modern logging practices by citing the ecological value of the remaining ancient forests and wilderness areas in North America. These ancient, or old-growth, forests and the wilderness areas within them represent irreplaceable natural systems. However, according to the Sierra Club, "Almost all the ancient forests on private lands have already been cut down. Only the national forests, managed by the U.S. government and owned by all Americans, have significant amounts of ancient forest left."

Half of those national forestlands are open to commercial logging under the supervision of the U.S. Forest Service, which grants permission on a yearly basis after receiving bids from private timber companies. Until the building boom following World War II, the logging that private timber companies conducted on public lands was held to approximately 2% of the total national harvest, by design, as the Forest Service was saving the the timber on national forestlands for the "future."

The future arrived much sooner than most thought it would. The logging private timber companies now do on public lands represents roughly 17% of the total national harvest. Today, roughly one square mile of America's ancient forests—mostly in Alaska, California, Oregon, and Washington—is being wiped out each week. The pace, some observers say, is accelerating because loggers want to maximize their profits before new, more restrictive laws are passed. Conservationists also claim that the logging industry is trying, through road building, to disqualify areas under consideration for wilderness designation. The rules under which the government manages its lands define wilderness areas as free of human activity. If a road is found on those lands, regardless of

continued on page 57

The creatures and natural landscapes shown on the following pages are offered in defense of preserving the wilderness. Though each living thing plays its practical and necessary role in maintaining the balance of nature, as these pictures reveal, the beauty and majesty of the wilderness may be its own best defense.

A large flock of Canada geese take wing after resting and feeding at one of the nation's federally controlled wetlands. Sights like this are a dramatic reminder of what will be lost if undisturbed areas of nature are destroyed.

Two red-breasted sapsuckers guard their tree nest. Without the protection of the forest, such birds would not be able to reproduce.

Small birds, such as this western bluebird, are not only beautiful but help preserve the balance of nature. Without them, human beings and their food supplies would be overwhelmed by insects.

From a branch above the water, a roseate spoonbill watches a family of common egrets. These long-beaked, long-necked birds pick their food from the mud just below the shallow water and could not survive without these marshes and swamps.

The majestic elk, a member of the deer family, photographed during winter in Yellowstone National Park.

The marmot is a chubby, short-legged, bushy-tailed creature that makes its home underground in the western areas of the United States. Small mammals of this kind require large territories to survive, and without them the larger predatory mammals would have nothing to eat.

This fawn, or young deer, is a grazing animal, and without large areas of virgin, grass-covered meadows, it would not survive to adulthood.

This picturesque little lake on Cape Cod, Massachusetts, is really a complex ecosystem supporting many species of fish, insects, birds, and plant life. Its peaceful appearance conceals a continuous struggle for existence that human activity could easily unbalance.

There is nothing quiet or pastoral about this dramatic view of the Flathead River near Glacier National Park. Though the landscape may look overwhelming, it is just as vulnerable to human activity as the smallest pond or marsh.

An aerial view of a portion
of the Florida Everglades,
the largest area of wetland
on the eastern coast of the
United States. A single
motorboat snakes its way
up a narrow channel in
the right foreground.

The western portions
of the United States
still have large areas
of undisturbed forest,
supporting many of
the rarest birds
and mammals of
North America.

continued from page 48

its origin, it becomes much more difficult legally to protect that land from commercial exploitation. Whatever the case, at the current rate, say experts, the ancient forests will disappear in 15 to 25 years. Forty percent of the country's ancient forests remain, but that percentage is shrinking fast.

Logging in the northwestern region of the United States—in Washington and Oregon—has already been restricted to some degree to protect the habitat of the spotted owl, which was recently listed as an endangered species. The U.S. Forest Service has called the owl an "indicator species," one whose disappearance would be a warning sign about the overall decline of the ancient forests. But logging officials and many of the industry's 600,000 workers ask how owls can matter more than jobs. Conservationists point out that if these ancient forests are harvested indiscriminately, those jobs will be in jeopardy even sooner.

The $54 billion timber industry is in the midst of a difficult transition. Thus far in its history, the industry has focused its thinking and its machinery on the big trees of the ancient forests. But those trees are a finite resource. At some point in the not too distant future, whether logging is done quickly or slowly, the big trees will be used up. The industry must soon turn greater attention toward smaller, "second-growth" forests, where some harvesting has already begun. This shift requires a significant investment in new machinery as well as a whole new approach to managing timber harvests on a sustainable basis. The desire to harvest the remaining big trees may be understandable in terms of short-term economic gain, but observers say the industry must focus more on the future. By redoubling its efforts to log in ancient forests, the timber industry is simply postponing the inevitable.

Conservationists also like to point out that the timber industry itself is responsible for job losses. One reason is the increased role of automated machinery in timber processing. Jobs have been eliminated even as production has increased by 50% since 1979. The new machines needed to handle the smaller logs of the second-growth forests will cut payrolls still further. Domestic mill jobs are also lost because roughly 25% of all the raw logs felled in the Pacific Northwest are sent overseas for processing.

Nevertheless, conservation-motivated restrictions on logging do present a serious economic issue. The U.S. Department of the Interior estimated that 28,000 jobs could be lost through measures undertaken to protect owl habitats. But conservationists insist that jobs could be saved if more labor-intensive methods of tree harvesting were employed, as opposed to using more machinery. Communities dependent on the timber industry will need financial help to retrain their workers and to diversify their economies. In spite of efforts to educate people about these complex issues, the simplistic "jobs-versus-owls" sentiment remains widespread.

A variation on the theme of "jobs versus owls" is seen in the conflict over the old-growth trees of Clayoquot (pronounced Clack-wit) Sound on Vancouver Island in Canada. There the two towns of Tofino and Ucluelet are pitted against each other in a bitter clash over commercial logging. As one resident said sadly, "One town is trying to destroy another town." Tofino's main business is tourism, and the hoteliers, restauranteurs, pleasure boat and campground operators, and others who make their living catering to visitors want the spectacular scenery to remain the way it is. One resident protested against the building of a logging road by taking up residence in a makeshift treehouse in a blasting zone. Her reward was an eight-day stay in a maximum security prison. Tofino residents are backed by various conservation groups.

Twenty-six miles away in Ucluelet, logging is the town's lifeblood, and the local forests have been heavily cut. The loggers here are an embattled community. Some recognize the need for preservation and for limits to be placed upon local logging but wonder what kind of jobs they could do instead. Generally, though, the industry wants to continue its practices unfettered by conservationist legislation. They are backed by powerful forestry firms such as MacMillan Bloedel Ltd. and Fletcher Challenge Canada Ltd. There is much at stake as well for the local government of British Columbia. The timber industry accounts for 10% of the province's $68 million gross domestic product.

The Clayoquot battle involves a debate over a complex question: What kind of economy is appropriate in an era of environmental crisis? In 1991, a task force representing all the major interests—the two towns, the logging companies, and the provincial government—issued recommendations that called for some selective harvesting but did not reduce the overall logging volume. Environmentalists complained that the panel's actions amounted to nothing more than lip service to conservation while logging continued. The environmentalists subsequently resigned from the task force amid tension and controversy.

Conservationists also direct a good deal of their criticism at the U.S. Forest Service. The Forest Service is supposed to administer its lands according to the principles of multiple use and "sustainable yield." This means harvesting trees in a way that ensures continued output for the future. Another way of saying this is that the logging industry must not cut down more trees than can be grown. But loggers are taking a much higher yield than is permitted—some 23% higher, according to the Forest Service's own figures. This is just one example, say conservationists, of how the Forest Service has bowed to timber industry pressure over the years. This has tipped the balance of forest use overwhelmingly toward logging and road building and away from multiple use and sustainable yield. This is disturbing enough on ecological principles alone, but it is especially distressing when analyzed in economic terms. According to the Wilderness Society and other environmental groups, most of the logging done on public lands loses money. The Congressional Budget Office has stated that "during fiscal year 1985 the Forest Service spent over $600 million more to administer its timber sales program and build logging roads than it received from sales of trees." Other studies have shown that between 1975 and 1985, losses from Forest Service timber sales amounted to $2.1 billion. According to the Wilderness Society, losses could reach another $2 billion by 1995. "Private companies that behave this way are called bankrupt," reports the society in its pamphlet *The Wasting of the Forests*. "They are driven out of the free-market economy. But the Forest Service has an advantage. It has access to the pockets of the taxpayers."

Timber industry representatives say that government subsidies help keep lumber prices down. In addition, Forest Service officials argue that timber harvesting should not be subject to the strict requirements of cost accounting and profitability. They also claim that road building helps prevent forest fires and increases opportunities for hunting and hiking. Conservationists reply that the industry already receives ample government tax breaks and that hikers prefer trails, not logging roads. Regarding future demands for wood, conservationists argue that this need could be met by private forests alone. All the land-owners would have to do is adopt intensive timber management practices—such as selective cutting instead of clear-cutting—and be satisfied with a more than reasonable 10% annual return on investment. If "below-cost" timber sales continue, this will not happen, and depletion of the national forests will continue un-abated. Furthermore, the timber industry has already mortgaged at least part of its future by prematurely harvesting some of the private, second-growth forests—trees that were to provide lumber some time in the next century. They are now trying to gain additional access to national forestlands to make up the shortfall.

Whereas Forest Service managers are experimenting with selective cutting and beginning to pay attention to new research about ecosystems that questions long-standing logging practices, this still represents only a fraction of Forest Service activity. The focus for conservationists remains the assault on old-growth forests—for example, proposed clear-cutting in Washington's Olympic National Park and in California's Shasta-Trinity National Forest. The economic argument made by con-servationists may be their most convincing. In its typical 50-year lifetime, a tree provides ecological benefits—the creation of oxygen, increases in soil fertility, the control of erosion, the control of climate, the provision of wildlife habitat, the recycling of water, the reduction of air pollution—that have been calculated to be worth $196,250. That same tree, if harvested and sold as timber, would be worth only $590.

AIR POLLUTION AND ACID RAIN

Thousands of forests and lakes in the eastern United States and Canada are being attacked by acid precipitation because they are located downwind from major industrial and urban areas. Extensive damage to lakes and trees in upstate New York's Adirondack State Park is brought about by pollutants lofted into the atmosphere from hundreds of miles away in Michigan, the heartland of the auto industry. Throughout the northeastern United States, sugar maple trees, producers of maple syrup, are in the early stages of a lethal epidemic, displaying symptoms such as stunted growth, bark fungus, and leaves that turn orange and fall off too early in the autumn. Instead of living to be 400 years old, many trees are dying at 65 or 70.

Acid rain damages tree leaves, reducing photosynthetic activity and literally starving the tree. It also changes the chemical composition of surrounding soils, weakening trees and making them more susceptible to disease, drought, and insect infestations. It is a threat not just to wilderness areas but to crops, buildings, and human health as well.

Technically, "acid rain" may come in the form of rain, snow, sleet, fog, or dry dust that is abnormally acidic. It is caused by the burning of fossil fuels such as coal, oil, and natural gas at factories and power plants; by the smelting of metallic ores; and by motor vehicle emissions—all of which produce carbon, sulfur, and nitrogen oxides that escape into the atmosphere. When combined with the water vapor naturally present in the air, these chemicals form weak concentrations of carbonic, sulfuric, and nitric acid. Some of the acidity in the atmosphere and in precipitation occurs naturally, but human activity, especially since the Industrial Revolution, has doubled the amount. In some regions, notably Europe and eastern North America, acidity levels have increased ninefold.

Restrictions on logging or other commercial or recreational uses of wilderness areas will prove futile as long as these areas continue to be subjected to this invisible air attack launched at long distance. Levels of emissions of these toxic waste products must be reduced. Many U.S. states, Canadian provinces, and other countries have begun to do this by requiring the use of improved smokestack technology and "scrubbers" that remove harmful pollutants from industrial waste gases. The introduction of lead-free gasoline has also helped, but critics contend that this is not enough. Conservationists point to alternative energy sources and increased recycling and conservation as effective long-term strategies to control acid rain.

OIL AND GAS EXPLORATION

The primary task of the petroleum industry, in its view, is to satisfy America's enormous appetite for inexpensive oil and gas. Thus it must constantly search for new sources and exploit them when promising finds are made. But what happens when the industry wants to explore in wilderness areas?

Nowhere does that question arouse more controversy than in the coastal plain of Alaska's Arctic National Wildlife Refuge. Conservationists call the area "America's last great wilderness." But the oil industry wants Congress to open the area

This oil-drilling rig on Avery Island, Louisiana, threatens the unique subtropical vegetation of this coastal area.

to oil and gas production. They say that the refuge is another Prudhoe Bay; that is, a vast reserve of oil and gas similar to the one that prompted the Alaskan oil boom of the 1970s. But according to the U.S. Department of the Interior, there is only a 1-in-100 chance that the oil industry will make such a find. Even if it did, the resulting annual yield would only be enough to satisfy a mere 2% of U.S. oil demand.

Conservationists are horrified at the prospect of oil industry activity in the region and have assigned the issue their highest priority. They point out that the infrastructure alone required for drilling and production—airfields, drilling pads, housing, sewage treatment plants, roads, and pipelines—would be extremely harmful to the environment. In addition, states the National Audubon Society, the industry's past record of exploration on the North Slope does not inspire confidence that exploration in the refuge would respect the wilderness.

For one thing, air and water pollution would undoubtedly become major problems. North Slope emissions of nitrogen oxides, a principal component of acid rain, are as high as those of Washington, D.C. There are an average of 1,000 oil and chemical spills per year on the North Slope. Another problem yet to be addressed is that of toxic waste disposal. In 1986, 110 million gallons of drilling waste, some of it radioactive, were pumped directly onto the tundra or sprayed on roads. Despite these and other hazardous practices, the Bush administration continues to support drilling and production in the Arctic Refuge.

The petroleum industry already possesses leases for oil and gas exploration on 60% of Yellowstone's National Forest lands. Elsewhere, it hopes to explore a potentially rich region of Montana's Glacier National Park, part of what is known as the

Overthrust Belt, even though wilderness areas would be disturbed. Attempts to explore the uninhabited island of St. Matthew in the Bering Sea were blocked by the courts. The island, a designated refuge and wilderness area, is one of North America's largest seabird nesting grounds.

The oil industry argues that wilderness designation "locks up" oil and gas resources. But according to a number of authoritative studies—by the U.S. Geological Survey, the Oak Ridge National Laboratory, and Leonard Fischman, one of the nation's foremost natural resource economists—areas already designated as wilderness or being considered for wilderness designation have little or no potential for producing oil or natural gas. Whether new, undiscovered reserves of oil and natural gas are vast or small or nonexistent, does it make sense to destroy remaining wilderness areas to get at them before the nation adopts higher standards of energy efficiency and resource conservation?

MINING

Like the petroluem industry, the mining industry also argues that wilderness designation "locks up" essential minerals. But most wilderness areas do not contain significant amounts of minerals because that is the way Congress drew the boundaries when the areas were established. Furthermore, those wilderness areas that do contain minerals represent a tiny fraction of U.S. land available for exploration and mining.

This does not mean, however, that wilderness areas are not threatened by mining. The General Mining Law of 1872 declares that the mining of uranium, silver, gold, and other metals is "the highest and best use" for more than 400 million acres of public lands in the western United States. According to the Sierra Club, "No other industry enjoys this exclusive protected status." The law, whose repeal is currently being sought, has tied the hands of environmentalists and allowed the mining industry to threaten some of America's most cherished wilderness lands.

On the edge of Grand Canyon National Park, uranium mining has caused so much soil erosion and land degradation that there is an increased possibility of flash floods, which would wash radioactive debris into the park's water sources. On the northern side of Yellowstone National Park, near Gardiner, Montana, a rise in world gold prices could revive a gold mine that would pollute the Yellowstone River. In Alaska's Denali National Park and Preserve, mining companies have built nearly 100 miles of unauthorized access roads across the tundra, according to the Sierra Club. Active mines in this area already produce levels of waste in local water supplies that routinely exceed minimum health safety standards.

The mining industry also blames environmentalists for job losses. As with the timber industry, however, automation is the primary culprit. More efficient machinery has made higher production possible with fewer employees.

OVERGRAZING

Overgrazing occurs when too much livestock feeds for too long on a given piece of land. Grasses are consumed down to their roots and do not regenerate. The ravaged soil is left vulnerable to erosion by wind and rain. If there is a prolonged drought, overgrazing can even create a permanent desert.

In the United States, conditions on public rangelands have improved since 1936, when the first surveys were conducted. By 1986, rangeland considered to be in "excellent" or "good" condition increased from 16% to 36%, while "fair" and "poor" rangeland decreased from 84% to 64%. Still, this means that nearly two-thirds of the country's federal rangeland rates as "fair" or "poor."

Public rangelands are administered by the Bureau of Land Management, which charges ranchers a fee for grazing rights. In 1981, that fee was set at 20% of market value by the administration of President Ronald Reagan. Ranchers who graze

Levittown, Long Island, New York. Suburban housing tracts, which have mushroomed all around the country in the last 30 years, require the clearing of large areas of land. Whatever grew here before has been lost forever.

on public lands pay one-fifth of what it costs on the open market for ranchers to graze their livestock on private lands. This govern-ment subsidy amounts to $75 million per year. If the money spent to maintain public grazing lands is included in the calculations, the government collects about $1 for every $10 spent.

Conservationists charge that this is more than bad economics; it is a "fire sale" of vast amounts of public land and wilderness. At the very least, they say, higher fees should be charged. They point out that 96% of the country's ranchers survive without subsidies or permits for public grazing. It has been suggested that the right to graze on public lands should be auctioned to bidders.

TOURISM AND RECREATION

America's national parks, forests, wildlife refuges, and the wilderness areas they contain are to some degree the victims of their own success. Visitors now flock in record numbers to crowded campgrounds, lodges, and hotels. They produce tons of sewage and waste material. Their cars, motorcycles, jeeps, off-road vehicles, boats, and campers create traffic jams that stretch for miles and pollute the air with their exhaust and the noise of their horns. In Grand Canyon National Park, flights by small planes and helicopters now number more than 50,000 per year. Easing the overall stress placed on the American wilderness by human activity will require extensive and controversial regulation of the very activities that bring such pleasure and enjoyment.

Dams provide inexpensive hydroelectric power, a clean and renewable source of energy. The reservoirs behind the dams, however, often flood thousands of acres of forest and destroy entire ecosystems.

DEVELOPMENT

Development is a broad term that applies to all manner of human enterprise. It includes the construction of new houses and factories, the conversion of swampland to farmland, and the building of shopping centers, golf courses, roads, and dams. All such projects represent an encroachment of civilization on wild areas.

The pace and style of development in Florida shows some of the things that can go wrong. The state's generally good weather and its appeal as a retirement haven have led to a population boom. The new residents require housing and other services. In the process of providing these services, the state's wildlife has suffered. The wading bird population has declined by a staggering 90% since the 1930s. Only 30 Florida panthers remain in a region where it was once the major predator; it is now the nation's most endangered large mammal. Even the American crocodile is threatened by plans for new condominiums and luxury hotels on a 12,000-acre parcel of land adjacent to the Crocodile Lake National Wildlife Refuge on North Key Largo. The Fish and Wildlife Service would like to buy land to serve as a buffer zone between the refuge and the new development, but it does not have the money.

Humans, too, have suffered. Development has disrupted the workings of the Everglades ecosystem, which encompasses Everglades National Park, Big Cypress Swamp National Preserve, and the Loxahatchee National Wildlife Refuge. Degradation of these areas means that floodwaters are not held back, and pollutants dumped into the water are not removed by the natural filtering action of the wetlands.

The problems of development are certainly not limited to Florida. In 1991, under pressure from home builders, farmers, and Congress, three federal agencies—the Environmental Protection Agency, the Department of Agriculture, and the Army Corps of Engineers—proposed that millions of acres of ecologically sensitive wetlands throughout the country be opened to development. The proposal comes just two years after the adoption of a stringent definition of the term "wetland" designed to avoid just such development. The action promises another bitter battle between conservationists and developers.

In 1988, a six-mile stretch of New Jersey beachfront along the Sandy Hook National Seashore was closed because medical waste materials were found washed up on the sands.

chapter 5

WILDERNESS AND THE LAW

In spite of all the current controversies, the United States has been for more than a century a world leader in the cause of conservation and wilderness preservation. The United States was the first country to create a national park—Yellowstone, in northwest Montana. The area's beauty and grandeur had been celebrated as early as 1807, when an explorer named John Colter returned from his travels with reports of geysers, hot springs, waterfalls, and natural areas boasting an incredible variety of wildlife. Some people in the East, unable to believe the descriptions of Yellowstone's wonders, dismissed the initial reports as fabrications.

It was not until 1870 that the suggestion was made to set the region aside as parkland. That year, members of an expedition to Yellowstone, upon experiencing it firsthand, became very excited about exploiting the area for commercial profit. One night one of the expedition members, Judge Cornelius Hedges, interrupted his companions' campfire reveries about the riches to be made with another idea: preserve Yellowstone as a national park. Two years later, to almost everyone's amazement, Congress passed the Yellowstone Act of 1872, establishing the world's first national park for the purpose of protecting and preserving the natural environment.

The Yosemite and Sequoia National Parks in California followed in 1890, largely the result of an effort spearheaded by John Muir, the leading conservationist of his time. Muir, a successful botanist and horticulturalist, had a deep, almost mystical love of nature. He spent great amounts of time hiking alone through California's Sierra Nevada mountain range, studying its trees, forests, and ecosystems. He also traveled abroad to survey the forests of Australia, Africa, and South America and wrote prolifically and eloquently about his feelings toward nature. One of the founders, in 1892, of the Sierra Club, Muir remains to this day a guiding spirit of the conservation movement.

Old Faithful Geyser in Yellowstone National Park. The growth of tourism and recreational activity threatens to overwhelm such landmark wilderness areas.

Even before Muir's words stirred the American public, the work of John James Audubon (1785–1851) did much to foster popular appreciation for the beauty of nature and wildlife. Audubon was an artist and ornithologist who specialized in painting beautiful images of America's bird life. His multivolume works, *Birds of America* and *Ornithological Biography*, were well received and brought him great success and acclaim in the United States, England, and Scotland. The National Audubon Society, another prominent conservation organization, was formed in his honor in 1905.

At the turn of the century, conservationists were of two minds about the progress they had made. On the one hand, additional national parks had been created as part of a national park system, among them Mount Rainier National Park in Washington State in 1899. The U.S. Forest Service had been established in 1905 to supervise and protect America's national forest reserves. But conservationists also felt that in a country as big as the United States, wilderness preservation had to be part of a unified national program. The movement was also divided into two schools of thought: use versus preservation. The former group believed that wilderness could be utilized without being abused. The latter disagreed, favoring strict limits on commercial activities on any land that was set aside as wilderness. These two groups clashed over a controversial proposal made in 1905 that called for a dam to be built on the Tuolumne River in a portion of the Yosemite National Park called the Hetch Hetchy Valley.

John Muir was one of many who were appalled at the thought of flooding and ruining the valley. He felt that the Hetch Hetchy was as splendid as Yosemite and opposed the project. His main opponent was Gifford Pinchot, head of the U.S. Forest

Service. Pinchot took a utilitarian stance: The dam would guarantee the supply of water and electricity for the speedily growing metropolis of San Francisco. After eight years of conflict, the dam was approved by Congress in 1913. A bitter Muir, reflecting on the defeat, wrote, "The destruction of the charming groves and gardens, the finest in all California, goes to my heart. But in spite of Satan & Co. some sort of compensation must surely come out of this dark damn-dam-damnation."

In 1919, Arthur Carhart, a forest service engineer, had been asked to analyze the Trappers Lake area in Colorado's White River National Forest in order to develop a plan for recreational development. Carhart liked what he saw so much that he recommended against development altogether. Instead of building summer homes, he wanted the area to be left in its wild, natural state. To Carhart's surprise, his highly unusual recommendation was accepted. It also brought him to the attention of Aldo Leopold, a forest service manager with responsiblity for much of the Southwest.

At the time of his first meeting with Carhart, Leopold's views on wilderness preservation were changing. He acknowledged that Pinchot's doctrine of use made good sense but felt that preservation thus far had been neglected. Carhart seems to have confirmed Leopold in his new beliefs, and the two found themselves in general agreement about the need for more wilderness preservation. Leopold had his eye on a 570,000-acre parcel of land in New Mexico's Gila National Forest, and in 1922 recommended its preservation. On June 3, 1924, the Gila Wilderness Area became the U.S. Forest Service's first administratively designated wilderness area.

Leopold once wrote that "a thing is right when it tends to preserve the integrity, stability, and beauty of the biotic community. It is wrong when it tends otherwise." This ethic formed the basis for the new science of wildlife management Leopold helped develop in the 1920s. Leopold was also a cofounder, in 1935, of the Wilderness Society. His book *A Sand County Almanac*, chronicling his acceptance of the conservationist's creed, is considered an environmental classic.

Two years after the designation of Gila National Forest as wilderness, the head of the U.S. Forest Service, Will B. Greeley, instructed Leon F. Kneipp, the chief of the Service's Division of Lands and Recreation, to survey other national forest areas. The first action of its kind in American history, the survey was intended to create an inventory of wilderness areas that could be officially preserved. Kneipp came up with 74 tracts of potential wilderness areas totaling 55 million acres. In 1929, Kneipp's work led the Forest Service to issue the "L-20 Regulations," which gave the chief forester the authority to establish "primitive areas" within national forests.

That same year, Congress enacted the Shipstead-Newton-Nolan Act, the first federal law in American history to protect a wilderness area. It targeted the Superior Primitive Area in northern Minnesota, protecting more than 1 million acres of interconnecting waterways. It was not until 1939, however, when the Forest Service issued the "U Regulations," that the word "wilderness" was used as an official designation for the first time.

Following World War II, government agencies began to change their attitudes and now looked upon their wilderness acreage as areas rich in materials and commodities that could contribute much to the great postwar building and recreation boom. Efforts were made to reclassify or declassify wilderness areas and open them up for development and exploitation. In 1950, Dinosaur National Monument came under attack. The proposed Echo Park Dam on Colorado's Green River would have destroyed part of the park, which straddles the Utah-Colorado border. Conservationists launched a campaign to save the park that involved all the major environmental organizations in the country and took six years of effort. It was the first time that a single wilderness area had been the focus of such a spirited, unified defense and marked the emergence of the conservation movement as a political force. The dam's construction was halted, but conservationists felt that they would exhaust themselves if they had to fight such battles over and over again with each and every assault on a particular wilderness area.

THE WILDERNESS ACT

Among the environmentalists who played an effective role in the campaign against the Echo Park Dam was Howard Zahniser, the executive director of the Wilderness Society. In 1951, though mired in the Echo Park struggle, Zahniser was able to set his sights beyond it and well into the future. Addressing the Second Wilderness Conference, held in California under the auspices of the Sierra Club, he issued a call to action that would refocus the energies of the conservation movement: "A bill to establish a national wilderness preservation system should be drawn up as soon as possible with the joint cooperation of the federal land-administering agencies and conservation organi-

Visitors to the Grand Canyon National Park say that sometimes the haze from air pollution is so severe that it blocks the view of the other side of the canyon.

zations. . . . Let us try to be done with a wilderness preservation program made up of a sequence of overlapping emergencies, threats, and defense campaigns! Let's make a concerted effort for a positive program that will establish an enduring system of areas where we can be at peace and not forever feel that the wilderness is a battleground!"

In 1956, following the Echo Park victory, Zahniser wrote the first draft of a wilderness bill. More than a dozen drafts later, the bill was introduced in the U.S. Senate by Hubert Humphrey of Minnesota and in the House of Representatives by John P. Saylor of Pennsylvania. The bill called for 50 million acres of federally managed, inviolate wilderness. Predictably, it met with great opposition. Commercial interest groups such as loggers, miners, and cattle ranchers felt that the bill threatened their livelihoods. But there was also bureaucratic resistance. The U.S. Park Service saw the legislation as an attack on its ability to manage wilderness areas in the national parks, and the U.S. Forest Service saw the bill as an infringement upon its jurisdiction and decision-making powers. The western states, traditionally against any kind of federal land management, lined up against the bill despite the support for it shown by some western legislators in both houses.

Conservationists realized that they would have to compromise. Zahniser himself recrafted the language of the bill to appease one special interest after another. In the seven years after it was introduced, the bill went through 66 different versions. Among the major alterations were the deletion of a provision creating the National Wilderness Preservation Council, the proposed oversight agency for the entire system, and the striking of a clause granting the president power to establish wilderness areas by executive order. A clause was added permitting grazing in wilderness areas where it had been the established pattern for many years. Another provision stated that wilderness areas were to be left open for mining until January 1, 1984. All of these changes pained conservationists. They foresaw, correctly, that compromise would dilute the overall effectiveness of the bill.

The bill was strongly supported by Stewart Udall, secretary of the interior, who is credited with winning the backing of President John F. Kennedy, who took office in 1961. On September 3, 1964, at a ceremony in the White House rose garden, President Lyndon B. Johnson signed into law the Wilderness Act of 1964.

Howard Zahniser did not live to see passage of the bill he had worked so hard to create. Worn out from his efforts, he died on May 5, 1964, at the age of 58. The law established a national wilderness system containing 9.1 million acres and directed the Forest Service to study its remaining "primitive" areas, and the Park Service and the Fish and Wildlife Service their respective holdings, to determine which of these should also be preserved as wilderness.

Nearly three decades later, the Wilderness Act itself gets mixed reviews. On the one hand, conservationists are glad to have protected what now amounts to 90 million acres of land and to have institutionalized the idea of wilderness preservation. They also recognize that they continue to face an uphill battle against commercial interests and flagging government commitment to its own laws.

A RARE CONTROVERSY

One of the conservationists' gravest disappointments about the Wilderness Act was its failure to create a government agency to monitor the National Wilderness Preservation System. Responsibility for enforcement of the new law remained where it was, divided among government agencies. The problem with this arrangement was illustrated in 1971, when the Forest Service conducted what it called a "Roadless Area Review and Evaluation" (RARE). The Forest Service performed the RARE study in compliance with the act's instruction to assess lands for wilderness availability. In doing so, however, the Service employed a stringent definition of wilderness that disqualified virtually all the land east of the Rocky Mountains.

Conservationists challenged the validity of the survey in the courts. Congress also became involved and in 1975 passed the Eastern Wilderness Act, which established 16 national forest wilderness areas in 13 eastern states. In 1978, Congress passed the Endangered American Wilderness Act, which established wilderness areas in the West and, in a rebuke to the Forest Service, put forth a much looser definition of wilderness so that more land would qualify. Far more extensive RARE II studies conducted in 1979 and the 1980s under the new definition of wilderness resulted in Forest Service recommendations for new wilderness areas. Conservationists, however, tired of fighting these battles every few years against recalcitrant government agencies, argue that some form of high-level administrative body is needed for the nation's wilderness areas.

Other disputes between conservationists and government agencies have centered around two laws passed in 1976, the National Forest Management Act (NFMA) and the Federal Land Policy and Management Act (FLPMA). The former charged the U.S. Forest Service with establishing 50-year plans for the management of each of its lands. It also limited logging and called for public review of Forest Service plans. But conservationists claim that the Forest Service is contravening the spirit of the NFMA by continuing to encourage exploitation of its lands for commercial purposes.

The FLPMA directed the Bureau of Land Management to decide which of its lands outside Alaska should be recommended for formal wilderness designation. But conservationists worry that the BLM, too, is so oriented toward development that much of its potential wilderness will be sacrificed. Lands in the wildlife refuge and national park systems have also been recommended for inclusion in the wilderness system, but Congress has yet to act on these proposals.

In 1980, President Jimmy Carter signed the Alaska National Interest Lands Conservation Act (ANILCA), declaring, "Never before have we seized the opportunity to preserve so much of America's natural and cultural heritage on so grand a scale." Indeed, the Wilderness Society has called ANILCA "one of the most ambitious conservation initiatives ever enacted." The measure created 104.3 million acres of national parks, wildife refuges, and other protected areas and was hailed as an almost revolutionary act of ecological wisdom and government foresight. Conservationists were thrilled at the newly designated 56.5 million acres of wilderness, which in a single stroke nearly quadrupled the National Wilderness Preservation System.

Still, serious threats now confront all of the lands covered by ANILCA. ANILCA called for a wilderness suitability review to be finished by the secretary of the interior within five years of its passage and for these recommendations to be forwarded to Congress within seven years. Both deadlines have passed with no action. The Wilderness Society has concluded that "the goals of the Alaska Lands Act have been twisted." One decade after its passage, the promises embodied in the last great piece of wilderness legislation remain unfulfilled.

The Brazilian rainforest, the most biologically diverse ecosystem in the world. This ecosystem is very fragile and is under attack by settlers, ranchers, miners, and those who would build more dams across the tributaries of the Amazon River.

T R O P I C A L   F O R E S T S

Every minute, 100 acres of the earth's oldest and most valuable ecosystem—the tropical rainforests of Africa, Asia, and Latin America—are cut, cleared, and burned. Over the course of a year, according to the Rainforest Action Network, roughly 125,000 square miles of this wilderness, an area roughly the size of Germany, will fall prey to the saw, ax, machete, bulldozer, or torch. Should this activity continue at current rates, experts say, almost all of the planet's tropical rainforests will disappear within the next 25 to 50 years, with potentially catastrophic consequences. Environmental organizations worldwide have made the fight against tropical deforestation one of their major concerns. It is the global wilderness issue.

Forests occupy approximately 30% of the earth's wildland. Rainforests account for two-thirds of all forests in the tropics. Rainforests once covered 14% of the earth's land surface, but today they cover less than 7%, and they are disappearing fast. Most of the rainforest has disappeared within the last 50 years, rapidly giving way before the ever-expanding and ever more damaging activities of human beings.

Tropical rainforests are found in lowland and lower mountain areas in a narrow band about 30 degrees north and south of the equator. In Africa, they are centered around the basin of the Zaire (Congo) River, along the Gulf of Guinea on the continent's central western coast, and along the eastern coast of the island nation of Madagascar. In South America, tropical rainforest covers the basin of the Amazon River, extending eastward through Brazil, westward to the foothills of the Andes Mountains, and northward to Colombia, Venezuela, Guyana, Suriname, and French Guiana. In Asia, rainforests are located in Myanmar (formerly Burma), western India, Laos, Malaysia, the Philippines, Sri Lanka, Thailand, and on the Indonesian islands of Borneo, Sulawesi, and Sumatra.

The world's tropical rainforests are one of nature's showpieces. Though their combined area is only about three-quarters the size of the United States (excluding Alaska), they are home to at least two-thirds of the earth's estimated 30 million plant and animal species. The rainforests of Southeast Asia's Malay Peninsula, for example, support 7,900 different flowering plant species and 2,500 native tree species. Though twice the size, Great Britain supports only 1,430 flowering plant species and 35 native trees. Bird species in Colombia number more than 1,550, more than twice the number of species found in all of North America.

This remarkable species diversity is just one of the reasons that the tropical rainforest ecosystem is considered vital to human survival. These trees and plants are the sources—sometimes the only sources—of one-fourth of the world's medicines, including those used to treat cancer, leukemia. and Hodgkin's disease, which affects the lymphatic tissue. The indigenous people living in the forests possess extensive knowledge about tropical plants and animals that could be important to scientists, but these people are also disappearing as the forests are destroyed.

Rainforests are also important for their huge resources of timber and vegetable materials such as waxes, dyes, tanning agents, rubber, and others chemicals used in hundreds of products, such as tires, toothpaste, and sunscreen lotions. The forests themselves control soil erosion and regulate the flow of rivers and streams, which in turn helps to avert or moderate droughts and floods. Through the process of photosynthesis forest plants draw in and store carbon, helping to moderate climate and reverse the trend toward global warming. One of the most serious consequences of the burning of tropical forests is an increase of 10% to 30% in total atmospheric carbon dioxide emissions.

CAUSES OF DEFORESTATION

Most of the causes of tropical deforestation are rooted in misguided economic policies and in the poverty that plagues the developing countries of Africa, Asia, and South America. Overpopulation, the desperate need for land to grow food or agricultural products for sale to other nations, commercial logging, the need to gather fuelwood, and the clearing of land for cattle grazing are all major causes of deforestation.

The soils of tropical forests are generally very poor, and only certain agricultural techniques will work over a long period of time without depleting the soils of their nutrients. The most successful technique is known as "slash-and-burn" agriculture, or shifting cultivation. A farmer clears a plot of land by slashing the vegetation and burning it. The remaining ashes help to fertilize the soil. The land is then used for several years, after which the fertility of the soil gives out and the farmer moves on to another plot of land and repeats the process. This leads to a kind of nomadic farming that is successful if carried out on a small scale, as it is with small groups of indigenous people moving through vast rainforests. Small areas of forest have time to regenerate and regain nutrients while the community is off working another patch of land. It may take 30 years or more for the soils to recover, and if the plots are big enough, allowing tropical rains to erode them before forest growth takes hold, they will never recover their fertility.

Shifting cultivation can work in areas of low population density, where there is enough land available for all those who need to farm. Unfortunately, overpopulation throughout the developing world means that more and more people are using slash-and-burn techniques on larger areas of forest. This exhausts the land and eventually renders it useless and vulnerable to erosion. According to the Global Tomorrow Coalition, misuse of the land in this manner "is responsible for 35 percent of the tropical deforestation in Latin America, nearly 50 percent in Asia, and 70 percent in Africa."

The growing of "cash crops" is another major cause of deforestation. They are so named because they are not grown as food for local consumption but for export to earn foreign currency. These crops, such as coffee and bananas in Central America and rubber and palm oil in Southeast Asia, are grown on huge plantations that require the clearing of large amounts of land. Not only does this destroy large tracts of forest, but by reserving large areas of prime agricultural land for a few commercial farming operations, many small farmers are driven off their lands, increasing the ranks of the poor who will have to slash and burn even more forest.

Commercial agriculture, as opposed to subsistence agriculture, also brings about the concentration of land ownership, contributing even more to deforestation. In Latin America, 93% of agricultural land is controlled by just 7% of the population. This leaves the rainforests as the only land available for the ever-increasing numbers of poor peasants who need to farm to survive. Redistribution of the land would ease pressure on the rainforests, but this is a controversial issue that threatens wealthy landowners and their political supporters.

Though it is not generally thought of as a cash crop, timber is by far the most lucrative rainforest resource, and the demand for exotic woods is rapidly destroying tropical forests. Indonesia earned $1.4 billion in 1986 from its timber exports. Loggers working illegally on the Philippine island of Palawan brought in $134 million in 1990. Also sharing in the business are large timber corporations from the United States, Canada, Western Europe, and Japan. Given the money to be made and the worldwide demand for timber, the pace of logging shows no signs of slackening. In some countries, logging for export is so extensive that domestic needs for timber cannot be met. In 1960, Nigeria was one of the leading exporters of tropical timber, but by 1985 it had become a net importer of forest products.

Rapid, unregulated logging has taken a devastating toll on the tropical wilderness areas of three continents and on the people who depend on the rainforests for survival. The rainforests in the Malaysian state of Sarawak, on the island of Borneo, have made Malaysia the world's leading timber exporter but are expected to be gone within a decade. On the Indonesian part of

This barren landscape in Nepal was once a beautiful wilderness area covered with forest. The country's need for foreign exchange has prompted the government to encourage the export sale of timber.

Borneo, careless logging methods contributed to a fire in 1983 that burned for four months, destroying $6 billion worth of timber across an area the size of Massachusetts and Connecticut combined. According to the Rainforest Action Network, logging in India has eradicated the subcontinent's great teak forests and reduced the forest cover in the Philippines by 90% since World War II.

Of course, such extensive logging would not occur if there were no market for tropical timber. That market is in the industrialized countries, which turn raw logs into housing materials, furniture, paper, and a host of other products. Japan leads the way, accounting for some 40% of tropical wood imports, followed by the United States, Great Britain, and the other countries of Western Europe. Experts say it would take a major change in consumption habits on the part of these countries to lessen the demand for tropical woods.

The gathering of fuelwood is another major cause of tropical deforestation. Wood and charcoal made from wood are the primary sources of fuel for cooking and heating for roughly half the world's population. Yet 1.5 billion people in 63 developing countries face what has been called a "fuelwood crisis." By the turn of the century, the shortfall is expected to confront twice as many people, some 3 billion in 77 countries.

People in rural areas looking for alternatives to wood often turn to animal dung or the residues of crops that have been harvested. But these are nutrient-rich substances that should be returned to the soil rather than burned. What appears to be a wonderful example of recycling instead contributes to topsoil degradation. City dwellers rely more on charcoal, considered attractive for its lighter weight and relative convenience. But the process by which wood is converted to charcoal halves the wood's original energy content, and the use of charcoal actually represents a dramatic loss in energy efficiency. In much of the developing world, the migration of peasants to the cities in search of jobs has only aggravated the fuelwood crisis.

Cattle ranching in tropical countries remains a major cause of deforestation. Much of the cattle ranching done in South and Central America uses techniques identical to slash-and-burn agriculture to clear land for grazing, and over time it also renders large areas of land useless. Encouraged by tax subsidies from local governments and a large demand from the industrialized countries for cheap beef for the pet food and fast food industries, cattle ranchers cleared and destroyed large areas of forest throughout Central and South America.

Since the mid-1980s, however, American dietary preferences have swung sharply away from beef. In addition, successful campaigns by conservationists as well as land degradation and warfare in El Salvador and Nicaragua led to a decrease in beef imports from Central America. Conservationists want all such imports stopped. They also want local governments to promise not to clear more rainforests for ranching.

GLOBAL LINKAGES

In late 1990, Chee Yoke Ling, the secretary of Sahabat Alam Malaysia (SAM), an environmental group that campaigns to save tropical forests, told *Maclean's* magazine: "Everyone talks about saving the rainforest, but they forget that the demand for tropical timber comes mainly from industrial countries. People in the West love to talk about recycling and switching to so-called green products, but they are not willing to change their way of life, which is based on unnecessary and wasteful consumption."

The linkage between the rich and poor nations of the world is playing an increasing role in discussions of global wilderness and environmental issues. Indeed, some analysts believe that with the end of the cold war between the United States and the Soviet Union, environmental issues will be the new source of international conflict.

There is no dispute about one revealing statistic: The industrialized countries of the world account for 30% of the world's population but consume some 70% of the planet's resources. That pattern has led the poorer countries to ask how governments and conservationists in the industrialized countries can criticize them for wanting to attain the same level of economic development by exploiting the only resources they have. Third World governments often bristle at what they perceive as interference in their internal affairs. Prime Minister Mahathir Mohammed of Malaysia said in 1990, "Unfortunately, the line taken by environmentalists is to lay the blame on poor countries and seek to force them to slow down their development in the interest of restoring the environment which the rich have polluted."

From the point of view of the industrialized countries, the developing countries are far from guiltless. For one thing, their populations continue to grow at alarming rates, taxing resources and the environment. According to the World Resources Institute, the developing countries' contribution to global warming is also on the rise and now accounts for 45% of all "greenhouse gas" emissions. (Greenhouse gases are those that prevent heat from escaping from the atmosphere, thereby contributing to global warming.) China has become the fourth largest producer of such emissions through its heavy reliance on coal.

Still, there is hope that the present crisis can be seen as an opportunity for international cooperation. The United Nations is currently considering three treaties on environmental issues. One would protect biodiversity by establishing a number of protected wilderness areas. Another would seek to limit exploitation of the world's tropical rainforests. The third would seek to control worldwide emissions of greenhouse gases. These will test the ability of developed and undeveloped nations to agree on actions that are, after all, aimed at saving the world for everyone.

Cattle ranching in Argentina, and throughout Central and South America, requires the clearing of large areas of forest and agricultural land and is in fact the single largest cause of forest destruction in these regions.

Another view of the Grand Canyon, showing how the Colorado River, over eons of time, has carved out a magnificently stark landscape.

CHALLENGES FOR THE 1990S

As the need for wilderness preservation becomes more and more urgent, the major conservation organizations of the United States have accelerated their efforts to expand the National Wilderness Preservation System beyond its current 90.7 million acres. They are lobbying Congress and state legislatures for the passage of wilderness legislation, monitoring the policies and actions of government agencies responsible for public lands, talking with corporations and industries about changing environmentally unsound practices, and educating the American people about the importance of wilderness preservation. All of these efforts have in common an attempt to create a social and political environment in which wilderness preservation has a high priority. It is an enormous agenda with much at stake.

Conservationists are hoping to establish new wilderness areas on Bureau of Land Management lands in the American West, while at the same time working to halt damaging logging operations in the ancient forests of the Pacific Northwest. They are fighting to have the coastal plain of the Arctic National Wildlife Refuge declared off-limits to oil and gas exploration.

Three important areas—the southern Appalachians, Greater Yellowstone, and the rural areas of northern New England—are felt to require greater protection. The Great Smoky Mountains of North Carolina dominate the southern Appalachian ecosystem, which encompasses 3.5 million acres and stretches into Georgia, South Carolina, Tennessee, and Virginia. It is home to the greatest number of tree species in North America and is considered one of the two most important centers for biological diversity in the United States. However, only 8.9% of the region is protected wilderness.

The 12-million-acre Greater Yellowstone ecosystem, with Yellowstone National Park at its core, covers parts of Idaho, Montana, and Wyoming—some of the wildest country left in the nation. Most of this land is administered by various agencies of the federal government and is threatened by timber harvesting and other activities permitted by those same agencies.

The northernmost parts of Maine, New Hampshire, and Vermont—some of the only wilderness left in the heavily populated Northeast—are mostly in private hands. Those owners, among them large paper and timber companies, have been selling extensive tracts for development.

Conservationists are also seeking extended protection to the Colorado Plateau. The canyon lands of the plateau, covering northern Arizona, southern Utah, and parts of Colorado and New Mexico, are one of the least inhabited areas of the United States. The largest concentration of national parks in the nation is here, but they are threatened by coal and uranium mining, dam construction, air pollution, and tourism.

Another goal of environmentalists is to create more wilderness areas within Glacier National Park and the national

Valley View at Yosemite National Park, near the Sierra Nevada in central California. Yosemite contains more than 1,000 square miles of wilderness and is visited by more than 2 million people every year.

forests of the Northern Spine in the Rocky Mountains. The Northern Spine runs from the center of Idaho to the northwest corner of Montana. Glacier National Park abuts this region, as do another Canadian national park and the Blackfeet Indian Reservation. It is a remote area under pressure from logging, oil and gas exploration, wildlife poaching, and off-road vehicles.

The California desert is another area in need of protective legislation. This desert covers nearly one-quarter of the state and is home to the world's largest Joshua tree forest. Heavy recreational use, especially by off-road vehicles, threatens the survival of this unique and sensitive environment.

The Florida Everglades and other wetlands throughout the country must be protected from further development. Excessive logging in Alaska's Tongass National Forest must be stopped. With 16.9 million acres, this is the country's largest national forest and contains the only temperate zone rainforest that is still largely intact, as well as the world's greatest concentrations of grizzly bears and bald eagles.

Internationally, reforestation efforts are being made in Australia, Brazil, Ethiopia, India, Mexico, Mozambique, and Tanzania, to name just a few countries. In the United States, the

A storm moves over the Florida Everglades, one of the nation's largest and most beautiful wetlands and home to many endangered species of wildlife.

Global Releaf program run by the American Forestry Association hopes to have planted 100 million new trees by 1992.

As individuals, people can help by cutting down on their use of forest products. It can be as simple as using cloth napkins instead of paper ones, reusing grocery bags, or using cloth or string bags instead. Newspapers and magazines can be recycled. According to the Sierra Club, an entire tree can be saved by recycling a stack of newspapers only four feet high.

Conservationists hope that all national parks, forests, wildlife refuges, and BLM lands will one day be considered part of one wilderness system and managed accordingly. More federal and state money for land acquisition, protection of natural resources, and scientific research must be allocated. Stronger federal legislation is needed to reduce the formation of acid rain and other toxic air pollutants. A compensation fund must be established to retrain workers who lose their jobs because of tigher regulation of timber and mining operations. Moreover, the country as a whole must learn to conserve energy and water and make greater use of renewable energy resources.

Despite the terrible damage already inflicted on the world's wilderness, the growing complexity of wilderness issues, and the rapid pace at which the wilderness continues to be destroyed, the effort to save wilderness areas must be made. It is shortsighted to think that industrial society can continue to function without the natural resources and biochemical recycling that forests and wetlands provide. Only when all the wilderness is gone will its importance be fully understood, and then it will be too late.

APPENDIX: FOR MORE INFORMATION

Environmental Organizations

Friends of the Earth
218 D Street SE
Washington, DC 20003
(202) 544-2600

Global Releaf
c/o The American Forestry
   Association
P.O. Box 2000
Washington, DC 20013
(202) 667-3300

Greenpeace U.S.A.
1436 U Street NW
Washington, DC 20009
(202) 462-1177

The National Audubon Society
950 Third Avenue
New York, NY 10022
(212) 832-3200

The National Parks and
   Conservation Associaton
1015 31st Street NW
Washington, DC 20007
(202) 944-8530

The National Wildlife Federation
1400 16th Street NW
Washington, DC 20036
(202) 797-6800

Natural Resources Defense
   Council
40 West 20th Street
New York, NY 10011
(212) 727-2700

The Nature Conservancy
1815 North Lynn Street
Arlington, VA 22209
(703) 841-5300

The Rain Forest Action Network
300 Broadway, Suite 28
San Francisco, CA 94133
(415) 398-4404

The Wilderness Society
900 17th Street NW
Washington, DC 20006
(202) 833-2300

The Sierra Club
730 Polk Street
San Francisco, CA 94109
(415) 776-2211

The World Wildlife Fund
1250 24th Street NW
Washington, DC 20037
(202) 293-4800

Government Agencies

Bureau of Land Management
Department of the Interior
18th and C Streets, Room 5660
Washington, DC 20240
(202) 208-5717

National Park Service
Department of the Interior
P.O. Box 37127
Washington, DC 20013
(202) 208-4747

FURTHER READING

Allin, Craig W. *The Politics of Wilderness Preservation.* Westport, CT: Greenwood Press, 1982.

Brown, Lester R. *State of the World.* New York: W. W. Norton, 1991.

Caras, Roger. *The Forest.* New York: Holt, Rinehart and Winston, 1979.

Carson, Rachel. *Silent Spring.* New York: Houghton Mifflin, 1987.

The Earthworks Group. *50 Simple Things You Can Do To Save the Earth.* Berkeley, CA: Earthworks Press, 1989.

———. *50 Simple Things Kids Can Do To Save the Earth.* Berkeley, CA: Earthworks Press, 1990.

———. *50 More Things You Can Do To Save the Earth.* Berkeley, CA: Earthworks Press, 1991.

Frome, Michael. *The Battle for the Wilderness.* New York: Praeger, 1974.

Hendee, John. *Principles of Wilderness Management.* Washington, DC: Government Printing Office, 1977.

Leopold, Aldo. *A Sand County Almanac.* New York: Ballantine, 1978.

McKibben, Bill. *The End of Nature.* New York: Random House, 1989.

McPhee, John. *Encounters with the Archdruid.* New York: Farrar, Straus & Giroux, 1982.

Muir, John. *Wilderness Essays.* Salt Lake City: Biggs-Smith/Peregrine Smith Books, 1980.

Thoreau, Henry David. *Walden.* New York: Signet, 1960.

Watkins, T. H. *John Muir's America.* Portland, OR: Graphic Arts Center Publishing Company, 1976.

The Wilderness Society. *A Vision for the Future of the Nation's Wildlands.* Washington, DC: The Wilderness Society, 1989.

Zaslowsky, Dyan, and The Wilderness Society. *These American Lands.* New York: Henry Holt and Company, 1986.

GLOSSARY

acid rain   Rain that has an abnormally high concentration of sulfuric and nitric acid; caused by industrial air pollution and automobile exhaust.

clear-cutting   Method of tree harvesting in which an entire stand of trees is removed in one harvest.

conservation   Planned management of a natural resource to prevent exploitation, destruction, or neglect.

deforestation   The process of clearing forests.

development   Use of undeveloped land for purposes such as housing, recreation, commercial logging, mining, military installations, shopping malls, tourist facilities, etc.

ecosystem   A community of organisms interacting with one another and with the chemical and physical factors within their environment.

global warming   The buildup of **greenhouse gases** in the atmosphere that is increasing the temperature of the earth's climate.

greenhouse gases   Gases such as carbon dioxide and methane that cause the buildup of heat in the atmosphere near the earth's surface.

habitat   The place where a plant or animal naturally or normally lives and grows.

multiple use   A land management policy that seeks to achieve a balance between the use of land resources such as timber and minerals and the protection of land as a watershed and wildlife habitat.

national forest   Protected public forests administered by the National Forest Service.

national park   Protected public land administered by the National Park Service.

off-road vehicle (ORV)   Also known as all-terrain vehicle (ATV); vehicles such as motorcycles and four-wheel-drive Jeeps capable of riding on unconventional surfaces such as dirt tracks, trails, grass, gravel, and tundra.

overgrazing   Consumption of rangeland grass by grazing animals to the point that it cannot be renewed because of damage to the root system.

ozone layer   An invisible layer of gas that shields the earth's surface by filtering out harmful ultraviolet radiation from the sun.

public lands   Lands owned and managed by the federal government.

rainforest   Woodland with an annual rainfall of at least 100 inches and marked by lofty, broad-leaved evergreen trees forming a continuous canopy; most often but not exclusively found in tropical climates.

reforestation   The action of renewing forest cover by planting seeds or young trees.

sustainable yield   The number of trees that can be harvested while still preserving a forest's future output; the harvesting of only as many trees as can be replaced.

topsoil   Surface soil, usually including the organic layer, in which plants have most of their roots.

watershed   A ridge or stretch of high land dividing the area drained by different rivers or river systems.

wilderness   A tract of land or a region, such as a forest or a wide barren plain, uncultivated and uninhabited by human beings.

wildlife refuge   Protected habitat administered by the Fish and Wildlife Service.

INDEX

Conversion Table

(From U.S./English system units to metric system units)

Length

1 inch = 2.54 centimeters
1 foot = 0.305 meters
1 yard = 0.91 meters
1 statute mile = 1.6 kilometers (km.)

Area

1 square yard = 0.84 square meters
1 acre = 0.405 hectares
1 square mile = 2.59 square km.

Liquid Measure

1 fluid ounce = 0.03 liters
1 pint (U.S.) = 0.47 liters
1 quart (U.S.) = 0.95 liters
1 gallon (U.S.) = 3.78 liters

Weight and Mass

1 ounce = 28.35 grams
1 pound = 0.45 kilograms
1 ton = 0.91 metric tons

Temperature

1 degree Fahrenheit = 0.56 degrees Celsius or centigrade, but to convert from actual Fahrenheit scale measurements to Celsius, subtract 32 from the Fahrenheit reading, multiply the result by 5, and then divide by 9. For example, to convert 212° F to Celsius:

$$212 - 32 = 180 \times 5 = 900 \div 9 = 100° \text{ C}$$

PICTURE CREDITS

AP/Wide World Photos: pp. 15, 40, 90, 93; The Bettmann Archive: pp. 20, 42, 64, 84; Chesapeake Bay Foundation: p. 37; Mike Floyd/National Park Service: p. 97; Grand Canyon National Park: pp. 12, 79, 94; Haugen/National Park Service: p. 98; H. Hobbs/Yosemite Collections, National Park Service: p. 53 bottom; Hood/Yosemite Collections, National Park Service: p. 50 bottom; Cal McCluskey/Bureau of Land Management, USDI: pp. 55 bottom, 56 bottom; National Park Service: pp. 49, 51, 54–55 top, 56 top; Betty Potts/Yosemite Collections, National Park Service: p. 50 top; Rainforest Action Network: p. 30; Maggie Steber: p. 18; TVA Knoxville, TN: p. 70; TW Recreational Services, Inc./Yellowstone National Park: pp. 52, 74; UPI/Bettmann: pp. 68, 72; US Fish & Wildlife Service: p. 35; USDA, Forest Service, photo by Jan Henderson: p. 29; USDI/Bureau of Land Management: p.26; H. Weamer/Yosemite Collections, National Park Service: p.53 top

A B O U T   T H E   A U T H O R

RICHARD AMDUR is a freelance writer and the author of three volumes in the World Leaders series published by Chelsea House: *Menachem Begin*, *Moshe Dayan*, and *Chaim Weizmann*. He has also written a biography of Golda Meir published by Fawcett/Columbine. His articles have appeared in the *New York Times*, *Cosmopolitan*, and other periodicals. He lives in Brooklyn, New York.

A B O U T   T H E   E D I T O R

RUSSELL E. TRAIN, currently chairman of the board of directors of the World Wildlife Fund and the Conservation Foundation, has had a long and distinguished career of government service under three presidents. In 1957 President Eisenhower appointed him a judge of the United States Tax Court. He served Lyndon Johnson on the National Water Commission. Under Richard Nixon he became under secretary of the Interior and, in 1970, first chairman of the Council on Environmental Quality. From 1973 to 1977 he served as administrator of the Environmental Protection Agency. Train is also a trustee or director of the African Wildlife Foundation; the Alliance to Save Energy; the American Conservation Association; Citizens for Ocean Law; Clean Sites, Inc.; the Elizabeth Haub Foundation; the King Mahendra Trust for Nature Conservation (Nepal); Resources for the Future; the Rockefeller Brothers Fund; the Scientists' Institute for Public Information; the World Resources Institute; and Union Carbide and Applied Energy Services, Inc. Train is a graduate of Princeton and Columbia Universities, a veteran of World War II, and currently resides in the District of Columbia.

CHATELECH SECONDARY
SCHOOL LIBRARY
DISCARDED

60984 81800